CUSTOMIZING
YOUR
PICKUP

About the Author

Mike Anson has been involved with trucks from as early as he can remember. "First," he recalls, "it was a green 1949 Chevy that belonged to my father. Then a '57 Ranchero with all the trimmings—including a 390 V-8 with three Holley carbs—was the big project. Currently, it's a jet black 1955 Ford F-100."

He has been involved in all phases of the automotive scene as a test driver, racing driver, and journalist. Anson has served as road test editor for *Road & Track*, automotive editor for *Newport Lift Magazine* and feature editor for *Four Wheeler* magazine.

No. 972
$8.95

CUSTOMIZING
YOUR
PICKUP
BY MIKE ANSON

TAB BOOKS
Blue Ridge Summit, Pa. 17214

FIRST EDITION

FIRST PRINTING—NOVEMBER 1977

Copyright © 1977 by TAB BOOKS

Printed in the United States
of America

Library of Congress Cataloging in Publication Data

Anson, Mike
  Customizing you pickup.

  Includes index.
  1. Motor-trucks—Customizing. I. Title.
TL 255.A57   629.28'8'3   77-25190
ISBN 0-8306-7972-3
ISBN 0-8306-6972-8 pbk.

Preface

Customizing pickup trucks has been a national pastime since the Model-A days. As this is written, the Ford F-100 pickup is the best selling vehicle in the country. Not the best selling truck—the best selling *vehicle*. What does that tell you?

It is doubtful that any of those new pickups will remain box stock for very long, for the pickup-truck owner is very special. Whether it's a new full-size pickup or a new mini-truck, each owner wants it to suit his needs and his tastes. The purpose of this book is to help you choose the customizing touches you want and then explain how to do them.

I want to thank the people who helped by providing material for this book: The Customizing Center in Newport Beach, Calif., and particularly Nancy Hoover, who made all that searching and hunting more fun; Recreational Vehicles Inc. (RVI) of Torrance, Calif., where Gary Wobig came through with vehicles and information to keep things going.

And thanks to the hundreds of customizers, both professional and not, who answered questions and provided information so the rest of us could have better looking custom trucks. Thanks to them all.

Blue sky, green lights and keep on truckin'.

Mike Anson

Contents

Chapter 1

Introduction to Customizing

A pickup truck is one of the most useful, versatile vehicles ever to come off an engineer's drawing board. It can serve as a utility vehicle, hauling everything from bales of hay to surfboards; it can be dressed up to serve as a Saturday-night cruiser, or it can do both. This versatility helps explain the success of the pickup.

Old pickups never die, they just keep on truckin' (Fig. 1-1). When is the last time you saw a pickup truck in a junkyard? Chances are you have never seen one there—they are too useful and too valuable. Pickups hold their value much longer than ordinary passenger cars, and since they are designed for hard use, they last much longer (Figs. 1-2 through 1-5). Even a wheezing, sick pickup with only two fenders and rags for tires can be worth as much as $1000.

But I don't have to tell you about all that—you already know, that's why you are reading this book. In the beginning was the Model T Ford and not much was done by way of customizing with it. The Model T was a workhorse. The first rumblings of customizing began with the Model A Ford (which is still a popular customizing vehicle today) and continued on through the 1930s. Things really began to pop in the early '40s but were interrupted by the war. After the war the customizing movement began again on a grander scale. Few pickups were immune to flames on the front, dropped front axles, Kelsey-Hayes wire wheels, and (yes, even back then) wider, larger tires (Fig. 1-6).

Fig. 1-1. Here is a real old-timer, complete with baggage trunk in the bed. Any model or make is fair game for customizing.

Fords were the most popular with Chevy running a distant second. In addition to doing his number with paint, grilles, wheels, and tires, the early customizer dropped the I-beam front axle for the lowered look. Often as not, he

Fig. 1-2. Everybody has to start somewhere. Mid-50s Fords are very popular with customizers. This '55 has a way to go—but you can be certain a dedicated customizer will have it looking good in short order.

Fig. 1-3. Chevy trucks are also quite popular. This 1951 would be a fine starter for a customizer. Don't be afraid of the older trucks—they just keep on running.

chopped the top, an expensive, time-consuming process in which a section is removed from the cab to lower it. Not only must the pillars be trimmed and welded, the windshield must be cut down as well. A chopped top is striking, but not too practical. Today the practice is pretty much limited to show trucks.

Any pickup is fair game for customizing, even the small mini-pickups from Japan. Datsun's Lil' Hustler caught on in

Fig. 1-4. A 1957 Chevy half-ton with the rear fender notched for the spare. These are also quite popular.

Fig. 1-5. Moving into the 60s we find a more boxy appearance. Handled correctly, the "square look" gives class to a custom.

Fig. 1-6. A nostalgic custom complete with flames, dropped axle, and custom wheels. Many hours of hard work went into this machine. Roof line extending over the windshield indicates a 1956 model.

12

1967 when Bob Carleton raced one in the Baja 1000. The popularity of the trucks astounded everyone, even the Japanese.

There are three distinct types of customizing: the nostalgic custom with a fond remembrance of things past; the off-road custom with roll bar, hyper-intensity lights, gobs of ground clearance and, sometimes, four-wheel drive; and the sanitary custom where the owner wants a conservative vehicle, clean but not trick.

All three aspects are covered in this book. But before we get started I want to point out that the instructions are written with a competent mechanic in mind. If a job sounds too difficult for your skills or your tools, then it probably is. Some high-technology modifications are included here, along with easy do-at-home mods. The bulk of these modifications are not difficult, but they do require some understanding of basic automotive terms and tools. Don't let this discourage you. For if you want a custom truck, there is nothing better than the feeling you get from having done it yourself. Get ready because here we go.

Chapter 2

Custom Showcase

Some of the wildest custom pickups gather every year at the Unnationals, an annual meeting of custom-truck, hot-rod, and custom-car enthusiasts held at the famous Knott's Berry Farm in Buena Park, Calif. Wandering around we caught some of the wildest and most sanitary trucks we have seen in a long time.

As you will see from the photos, most of the trucks are early Fords, the "in" brand. If you can't afford (they are getting expensive) a vintage Ford, don't be discouraged—any pickup can be customized effectively if you have a good eye, good taste, and a good feel for just what customizing is. You can take an ugly mid-40s Dodge and make it look good if you really want to. Take a look on the following pages (Figs. 2-1 through 2-8) and see just what will work for you and your truck.

Fig. 2-1. Henry Ford certainly never thought one of his would turn out this way—full custom complete with blower and four-barrel carb.

Fig. 2-2. How's this for plush? A television set and a crushed velvet interior.

Fig. 2-3. When customizing your pickup don't overlook the bed. This owner used wood and covered it with a protective coat of resin—it looks great.

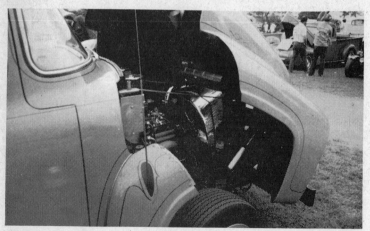

Fig. 2-4. Tilt front ends, for easy access to the engine, are popular on early Fords. It's expensive and complicated but the result is worth the effort.

Fig. 2-5. What to do with the license plate has always been a problem. Here is one solution—frame the plate in wood. It's a nice touch.

Fig. 2-6. This truck features extensive undercarriage work, including the addition of a Jaguar "monkey motion" rear end.

Fig. 2-7. An outstanding engine compartment. Note the gauges for tuning and the hydraulic cylinder to operate the tilt-front end.

Fig. 2-8. Trucks reworked by RVI include a mirrored headliner (Mylar, not glass) and sunroof. Note the aircraft-type lights, an idea borrowed from the vanners.

Chapter 3
Mini-Truck Spotlight

Stumped for customizing ideas for your mini-truck? Fear not. We took a look around the custom car shows and came up with a selection of tip-top mini-trucks (Figs. 3-1 through 3-8). Don't be overwhelmed by these professional examples; everybody has to start someplace. Many of these trucks, while on the show circuit, are still driven regularly on the street. Many of the ideas can be applied to the full-size trucks as well. Keep on customizin'.

Fig. 3-1. Trunkin' Tootie—Bob Bond's custom is an eye-opener for LUV lovers

Fig. 3-2. Yellow fever is a Datsun with red-orange flames following through to the rear, cartoon on hood, and features custom lights inset into the grille.

Fig. 3-3. Crystal Blue Persuasion carries blue and white colors blended to make the finest custom paint job we've seen.

Fig. 3-4. Air scoop on this show truck blends into the fender flairs and carries flush-mounted driving lights. Restrained striping on the hood accenturates the square lines and topside power scoop.

Fig. 3-5. Wild flame job on this show car with a permanent shell gives the impression of movement.

Fig. 3-6. Remember the Morris Minor! This one, in bright orange paint, was one of the cleanest on the L.A. show circuit. Padded vinyl bed was great for carrying home the trophies.

Fig. 3-7. Rear view of the Morris and that padded bed.

Fig. 3-8. A few simple items will dress up a stock Datsun in a hurry. This one has a chromed bumper guard, wide tires on mags, sidepipes, and light striping work.

Chapter 4

What's New

Today you don't have to break out the old welding torch to give your truck a customized look. Thanks to the specialty manufacturers, there are hundreds of ready-made bolt-ons that can add flash and utility to your four-wheeler. We've picked out some of the newest and most interesting designs we've come across for the following pages (Figs. 4-1 through 4-5).

Fig. 4-1. Tinted bubble windows—these cool, tinted, and distortion-free rear windows add a touch of custom to any pickup. DOT-approved, the windows install easily, using the existing rubber gasket. The manufacturer claims that the smoke tint filters glare and lowers in-cab temperatures. Available from Desert Dynamics, 13720 E. Rosecrans Ave., Santa Fe Springs, CA 90670.

Fig. 4-2. Double-hoop roll bars add style and protection to any mini-pickup. Constructed of mandrel-bent, seamless steel tubing, these roll bars are secured by large flanges and SAE grade No. 8 bolts. Check with the folks at True Radius Bending, 412 N. Nopal, Santa Barbara, CA 93103.

Fig. 4-3. These quality roll bars (1 3/4-inch diameter for minis and 2 inches for full-sized pickups) feature dual light-mounting tabs and are armored with a baked-on metallic coating. Available from Jackman Wheels, 1000 N. Johnson Ave., El Cojon, CA 92020.

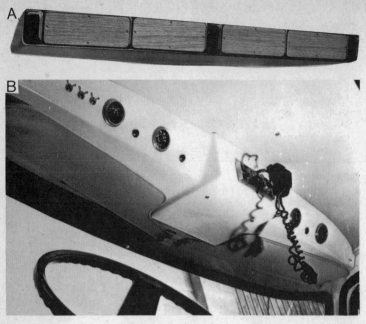

Fig. 4-4. An overhead console is a handy place for gauges or a CB radio. Mini-truck consoles, shown in view A, can be supplied by Flite-Tronics, 2221 Empire Ave., Burbank, CA 91504. These units are wood-grained for a painless match with any interior. Full-sized pickups benefit from injection-molded consoles (view B) from Hooker Headers, 1032 W. Brooks St., Ontario, CA 91761.

Fig. 4-5. This fiberglass spoiler and nerf-bar combination is designed to fit the Chevy pickup. For more information, contact Hooker Headers, 1032 W. Brooks St., Ontario, CA 91761.

Chapter 5

The Trucks

"The light-duty truck market—pickups, vans, recreational and utility vehicles—is booming, and industry sales are expected to exceed three million trucks in 1976 with an even larger sales figure expected for 1977" said James T. Riley, sales manager for Chevy. Truck manufacturers realize that the demand is going up and up. Millions of Americans are discovering that a truck can do two jobs: It can work and it can provide comfortable transportation. We know about a third use—pickups are great for customizing.

Surprisingly enough, the people who build the trucks know that too. Sometimes it takes them a little while to get in gear, but they realize that customizing is an important area. For that reason most of the major manufacturers have introduced semicustom packages for their pickups (Figs. 5-1 through 5-3). Can you believe a pickup rolling off the assembly line with stripes, roll bar, grille guard, white-spoke wheels, white-letter tires, and a trick interior? Well, it's happening.

"Much like the 'muscle cars' of the 60s," Riley continued, "pickups have become a symbol of a person's individuality. Among pickup trucks, the personal-use factor is most evident in the sales growth of the sporty short-box, step-side trucks. Sales of these units have *doubled* compared to sales of a year ago." That's strong stuff from the corporate side. The folks at the factory know we are out here.

James E. Conlan, GMC sales manager knows about pickup-truck popularity too. "The increase in leisure time

Fig. 5-1. GMC will build 500 replicas of this Indianapolis pace truck.

because of earlier retirements, additional vacation time, etc,. means people have more time for recreational activities," said Conlan. "The pickup truck has been playing a growing role in an expanding recreational-vehicle market. Styling in pickups—both interior and exterior—has improved over the past few years. This has resulted in many people buying a pickup as a second or third car.

"Pickups have the capability to serve both work and pleasure needs. In fact, a pickup parked in a driveway is a status symbol. Pickups today look good, are quiet and comfortable and come with options such as air conditioning, power brakes, power steering, and luxurious interiors," Conlan continued.

Fig. 5-2. The Sarge is another semicustom from GMC, with rails, dished wheels, white-letter tires, and adhesive stripes.

"Pickup-truck sales, like other light-truck models, parallel the demand for passenger cars. When car sales declined during the past two years, pickup sales also were off. Now pickup sales are exceeding the upturn in the car market. Light trucks, composed primarily of pickups, account for more than 85% of the total truck market. They are used in business and for personal transportation and recreation. One of six U.S. households owns at least one truck. About 45% of light trucks are used for personal transportation, 35% for business, and 20% for both business and personal use."

Okay, so the people who build and merchandise pickups know we are out here. But what are they doing for us?

In addition to the semicustom kits mentioned previously, manufacturers have made serious sheet-metal modifications to whet the appetites of custom-truck fans.

The most striking the mods is the return of the step-side bed. Until the late 1950s all pickups were step-sided; that is, the rear fenders were outboard of the bed. While hardly space-efficient, step-side styling enhanced the wheels and left an uncluttered cargo bay. Slab-side pickups were considered a great advance. The fenders are inboard, so that the exterior sides of the bed are flat. While the additional bed space is welcomed by commercial users, the boxy appearance of these vehicles is nothing to get excited about. Customizers scrounged junkyards in search of early step-side beds. Just as the supply was exhausted, Detroit came to the rescue with a new generation of step-sides (Fig. 5-4).

Mini-truck manufacturers have been more conservative than the Americans, possibly because the home market is still

Fig. 5-3. Dodge never built such a pretty Power Wagon. Note the agressive tread profile, wild paint, and double-barreled roll bar.

A

B

Fig. 5-4. Step sides are back. GMC features spoked wheels and breakline styling (view A). The Dodge Warlock (view B) is striped, staked, and slick.

Fig. 5-5. The LUV is built by Isuzu, a well known manufacturer of heavy trucks and diesel engines. Good basic lines and generous wheel cutouts make it a natural for customizing.

30

Fig. 5-6. The boss mini, outselling all others. Datsun offers short- (view A) and long-chassis versions, as well as the King Cab (view B).

Japan's largest. Sheet-metal changes are few. The real progress is in interiors, engines (Courier) and in the new-generation five-speed transmissions (Figs. 5-5 and 5-6). Fifth gear is an overdrive, resulting in better highway mileage and extended engine life. Datsun has introduced a long-wheelbase chassis and the King Cab for greater legroom and under-key storage capacity.

Chapter 6

Wheels & Tires

Custom wheels and fat tires transform a pickup from stocker to semicustom in one fell swoop. If you select wisely you will improve both braking (important in a pickup because of the forward weight bias) and the cornering performance.

TIRES

Everything you need to know about a tire is written on the sidewall (Fig. 6-1). You will find:

- Style
- Manufacturer
- Type
- Material—nylon, fiberglass, or steel
- Size
- Load range, including maximum load and maximum air pressure
- DOT (Department of Transportation) certification and codes, plus date of manufacture

Style

There are three basic tire styles—whitewall, blackwall, and raised-letter blackwall. As for the style name, let your imagination go—the people who name the tires do. They may be called anything from Tiger Paws to Fat Weenies. For customizing, wide-configuration, raised-letter blackwalls are the most popular.

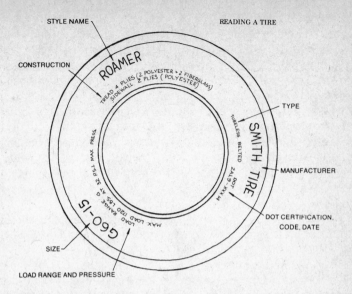

Fig. 6-1. Most information you need to know is on the sidewall. (Courtesy Customizing Center.)

Type

The least expensive type is the old-style bias ply in which the plies, or layers, of cord run at angles across the tread (Fig. 6-2). This design gives a relatively smooth ride at moderate speeds. The sidewalls are tough enough to scuff the curb a few times without major damage.

Belted-bias tires are a compromise between bias- and radial-ply tires and represent a stopgap measure by U.S. tire makers to stem the tide of imported radials. As you can see

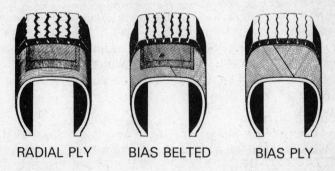

RADIAL PLY   BIAS BELTED   BIAS PLY

Fig. 6-2. Three types of tire construction are used today. (Courtesy Customizing Center.)

33

from the drawing, a belted-bias tire is simply a bias-ply tire with reinforcing belts to hold the tread flat on the road. The benefits are better traction, handling, and mileage. The disadvantage is a slightly harsher ride. Some manufacturers have experienced tread-separation problems, although this seems to be a thing of the past.

Most experts consider the radial the best tire available. The cords, usually made of steel, run at right angles (radially) to the tread. Radial tires offer superior wet-weather traction, improved braking and exceptional mileage. On the debit side, radials are narrower than belted-bias 70, 60, and 50 series tires, are expensive, particularily in the larger sizes, and are harsh-riding at low speeds.

If you are going for looks and some performance, choose a wide, belted-bias tire; if you are going for performance alone, purchase the widest radials you can find.

Whatever type you choose, don't mix them. If possible have the same type of tire (maker and tread design) at all four corners of the truck. If you are stuck with different types, pair the radials at the rear, never at the front, and never use a single radial with three other types, except in an emergency.

Construction

The carcass, or foundation, of a tire is made up of layers of fabric strands imbedded in rubber. Each layer is a ply and the strands are called cords. There are many types of cord material; the most common is nylon. While nylon is tough and gives long life, it does have the disadvantage of "flat-spotting" in cold weather. The tire bumps and thumps until it rounds out with heat. Rayon is the cheapest and most fragile cord material; avoid rayon tires like the plague. Polyester is a relatively new synthetic that resists flat spots and offers long life. Fiberglass is said to give a smooth, quiet ride, but I have found this not to be true in many cases. Employees at tire stores refer to fiberglass-belted tires as "fiberglass hammers" because of customer complaints. For strength and durability, steel is the winner—a steel-belted radial is the best tire available today.

Tire Size

Tires are listed by two sizes: The nominal section width and the nominal wheel diameter. Section width is listed first, followed by wheel diameter. Section width refers to the sidewall-to-sidewall measurement with the tire inflated, but not under load (Fig. 6-3). Tire width is often confused with

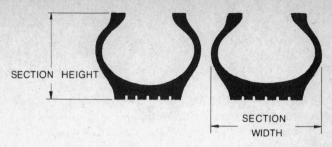

SECTION HEIGHT

SECTION
WIDTH

Fig. 6-3. Section height is the distance from the tread to the bead; section width is the distance across the widest portion of the tire. Both are measured with the tire inflated but carrying no load. (Courtesy Customizing Center.)

section width, but the two are very different. Tire width is the measurement of the tire beads where they seat on the rim and is usually narrower than the section width.

Until recently tire sizes were listed by section width and rim diameter. For example, 8.25-15 indicates a section width of 8 1/4 inches and 15 inch diameter rim. Most large truck tires are still marked this way. Light-truck and passenger car tires are sized by the aspect ratio, the ratio of the tire's section height to section width. As shown in Fig. 6-3, section height is the distance from the tread to the bead seat with the tire inflated, but not under load. To determine the aspect ratio, divide the section height by the section width.

The lower the number the wider the tire (Fig. 6-4). Some years past, series 83 tires—tires whose section height was 78% of section width—were popular. Today these narrow tires have been replaced with series 78 and 70 on passenger cars. Sports models often use series 60 tires. Pickup trucks usually have room in the wheel wells for series 60 series and ultrawide series 50 tires.

Before you mount series 60 or 50 tires on your pickup, you should be aware of several facts: Wide tires may develop wear patterns that cannot be explained by out-of-balance, worn shocks, or wheel misalignment. Tire experts are at a loss to explain why some wide tires give good tread life, while others go bald in less than 15,000 miles.

Ultrawide series 50 tires look good, but wear out quickly. Another consideration is steering effort. If your truck does not have power steering, you will find that wide tires increase steering effort dramatically at low speeds. In addition, the increased rolling resistance of the wide tire puts an additional

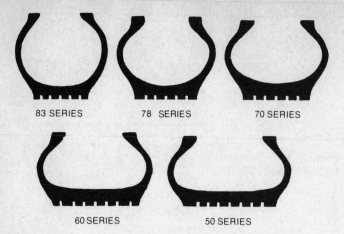

83 SERIES 78 SERIES 70 SERIES

60 SERIES 50 SERIES

Fig. 6-4. Tires are available from ultra-skinny to ultra-fat. For customizing your pickup, you will be interested in series 60 and 50. (Courtesy Customizing Center.)

load on the suspension and drive-line components. Check for adequate wheel-well clearance, recognizing that the tire must clear with the suspension collapsed. Never jack up the suspension to make room for oversized tires, since this raises the truck's center of gravity and increases body lean in turns.

Fat tires can affect the handling in unpleasant ways. For big tires improve traction and the truck feels as if it is a sports car—but it isn't. It is still a truck. Too often the unthinking driver will go too deeply into a corner, counting on his tires to see him through. They might, but under certain conditions wide tires can flip the truck.

This happened to me during a skid-pad test of a mini-truck shod with wide tires. The truck was behaving beautifully. Suddenly, as I was going around the 200-foot circle the truck

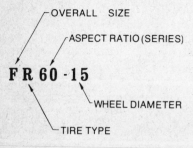

OVERALL SIZE

ASPECT RATIO (SERIES)

F R 60 · 15

WHEEL DIAMETER

TIRE TYPE

Fig. 6-5. This designation is for a size F radial with an aspect ratio of 60 sized to fit a 15-inch rim. (Courtesy Customizing Center.)

started to crab, to hop sideways—a sure sign of impending rollover—and flipped. Fortunately no one was hurt, but the episode brings home the point about overconfidence in truck suspensions.

Overall Size

Tire manufacturers use a letter designation for the overall size of the tire; the smaller the tire the earlier the letter appears in the alphabet (Figs. 6-5 and 6-6). A tire designated C70-14 is smaller than one designated F70-14. Since the load range is also designated by letter, it is important not to get the two confused. The law in some states limits tire-size increases to two letter sizes. For instance, if your Chevy was delivered with F70-14 tires as standard equipment replacement tires could be no larger than H70-14, assuming you stayed with OEM rims.

DOT Codes

The final digits of the DOT code stamped on the sidewall are the date of manufacture. For example, if the digits are 027 or 27, the tire was manufactured in February, 1977. The DOT code also identifies the tire manufacturer, something that may be of interest if you buy a house-brand tire. The Tire and Rim Association publishes a booklet that translates these and other code numbers called *Who Makes It Where*. For a copy send $1.50 to Bennett-Garfield Publications, 2119 Route 110, Farmingdale, NY 11735.

LOAD RANGE – PLY RATING COMPARISON TABLE

LOAD RANGE	EQUIVALENT PLY RATING	LOAD RANGE	EQUIVALENT PLY RATING
A	2	H	16
B	4	I	18
C	6	J	20
D	8	K	22
E	10	L	24
F	12	M	26
G	14	N	28

Fig. 6-6. More letters, this time for load ranges. Range D (8 ply) is about the limit for the street. Ranges E through N are intended for construction and agricultural tires. (Courtesy Customizing Center.)

Air Pressure

Maximum allowable air pressure is stamped on the tire. In most cases 32 psi (pounds per square inch) is the limit. This is not the recommended pressure, but the maximum pressure for greatest load-carrying ability. Often there is a conflict between the tire manufacturer's recommendations and the vehicle manufacturer's. The car maker wants a soft ride and tends to give a pressure recommendation that is too low. The tire manufacturer raises the pressure for maximum tread life.

What's the solution? Start with a recommended pressure and watch the wear pattern develop. Wear in the center of the tread indicates overinflation. Wear on the outside edges means underinflation.

Keep the pressure on each axle the same. However, it is possible to improve pickup-truck ride and handling by varying the tire pressure between the front and the back. The author's Ranchero responded best with less air in the rear tires—this eliminated rear-end hop during braking and gave a good all-around ride. Remember to add air when you carry loads.

Tread Patterns

Pickup trucks are usually fitted with one of three tread patterns: Passenger-car, truck, or off-road. The passenger-car pattern is popular for series 60 and 50 tires. This tread pattern develops good traction on pavement, performs adequately in the wet, and is quiet.

Truck patterns are designed for long mileage with little consideration for driver comfort. They do not do as well in the rain as the passenger-car treads, but they usually have eight plys and a large load-carrying capacity.

Off-road tires have deep, well separated treads, to cope with sand, snow, and mud. Off-road tires do not perform well on the street where they slip, howl, and whine.

Select the tires you need as determined by the use your pickup will see. If you rarely haul heavy loads and you stay clear of the desert and the mountains—go for the passenger-car tread design.

WHEELS

The staggering variety of custom wheels makes selection difficult. Do you choose plain-Jane reversed wheels, white-spoked steel, slotted aluminum alloy, or two-piece chrome-spoked wheels? Ultimately the choice is a matter of esthetics, of which pattern looks best on your particular truck.

My purpose here is to describe what is available and to point out some of the features you should look for (Fig. 6-7).

First let's clarify the term "mags." Today mags means alloy wheels. The term is a carryover from racing wheels which are made of magnesium. Magnesium construction is impractical for street wheels. True mags must be X-rayed every six months to detect fatigue cracks and will crumple if run into a curb or other obstruction. Wheels designed for street use are made of steel on aluminum.

When selecting wheels, one of the first things to look for is the SEMA sticker; it means the wheels have been tested and meet safety specifications established by the Specialty Equipment Manufacturers Association. The quality of cast wheels is high enough that many manufacturers guarantee the wheel to hold a tubeless tire. However, sometimes a porous casting will slip through and you will have a leaker. In that event get a replacement wheel or use a tube in the tire.

Types

For the most part, aftermarket wheels are one-piece aluminum-alloy castings or two-piece constructions of aluminum and steel. One-piece wheels are die cast (usually in Japan) and then machined. Two-piece wheels are less expensive because they are built up from stock rims with new center sections riveted or welded in place.

Pickup trucks can be fitted with stock-appearing wheels that have been widened to accomodate series 60 and 50 tires. The process involves cutting the centers out of the stock wheels and welding them to new, wide-section rims. The wheels are painted the same color as the truck and trimmed out with OEM or baby-moon hubcaps. These wheels are very popular with the older customizer who remembers that this was the style of the 50s.

When selecting a set of wheels you must consider these factors:

- Bolt pattern
- Type of brakes (disc calipers often present an interference problem)
- Rim width
- Rim diameter
- Offset
- Style

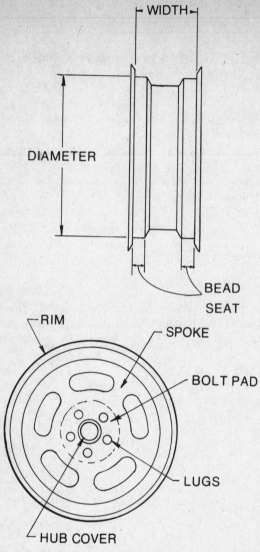

Fig. 6-7. Learning the wheel nomenclature is helpful when selecting wheels for your truck. (Courtesy Customizing Center.)

Bolt patterns differ between manufacturers although there is more uniformity with trucks than with cars (Fig. 6-8). Five-bolt patterns will vary, but once you get into six- and eight-bolt patterns you will find the bolt-circle diameters are the same. Most American truck makers use the same Budd axles and spindles and, as a result, bolt patterns are the same.

If you want to swap rims from one truck to another, count the lugs, measure the bolt circle, and check for interference. Do not attempt to modify them yourself. Adapters are available to take care of most mounting problems and spacers can be used for caliper clearance.

Pickup trucks have ample wheel-well clearance. Full-sized trucks can usually be fitted with tires as wide as 10 inches in the rear; mini-pickups can usually take an 8-inch tread.

Offset

Offset refers to the location of the wheel-mounting surface in relation to the wheel centerline (Fig. 6-9). Most custom wheels are built with negative offset to increase the depth of the wheel as seen from the street side. This is done by moving the mounting surface closer to the brake drum for that deep-dish effect. Negative offset increases the track and sometimes causes interference problems. Extreme negative offsets will overstress the wheel bearings. Positive offset is used when the fender lip restricts outward movement (as is sometimes the case with mini-trucks).

MATCHING WHEELS AND TIRES

In order to work together, wheels and tires must be matched. Installing a 10-inch wide tire on a 6-inch rim will crown the tread in the middle. Handling will be erratic and dangerous; traction will be almost nonexistent.

The American Tire & Rim Association recommends that rim width be at least 75% of the tire's section width. That means if your tires have a section width of 8 inches, the minimum rim width should be 6 inches. Experienced street rodders go further and believe that the rim should be 1 inch narrower than the secton width. If you stay close to this rule you should have no trouble matching the wheels and tires.

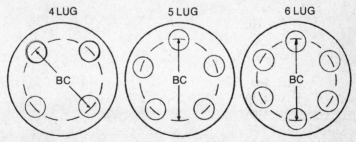

Fig. 6-8. Bolt-circle diameter is the center-to-center distance between opposed lugs. (Courtesy Customizing Center.)

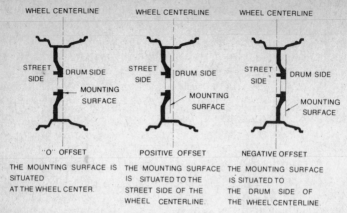

Fig. 6-9. Wheel offset is critical for steering and wheel clearance. Most specialty wheels feature negative offset for appearance. (Courtesy Customizing Center.)

RIMS

The drop center is the depressed portion of the rim between the bead seats (Fig. 6-10). The heavier the tire, the shallower and wider the depression must be. Standard drop centers are used on wheels up to load range. Large pickups with the eight-bolt hubs and eight-ply tires come with semi-drop-center rims. Unless you run a heavy camper, semi-drop-center rims are not necessary.

MOUNTING TUBELESS TIRES

As with anything else, there are two ways to mount tires—the right way and the wrong way. Mounting tires on custom wheels without doing violence to the chrome or the paint requires special precautions.

Start by removing the stock wheel and inspecting the brake drum or caliper for clips, washers, or debris that would

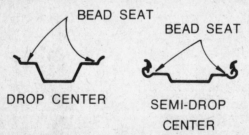

Fig. 6-10. Rim profile is determined by the tire size. Most pickup trucks use the standard drop-center rim. Split, or semidrop-center, rims are used on heavy-duty applications. (Courtesy Customizing Center.)

interfere with the new wheel. Discard the spring clips on Chevrolet and Ford drums. Make a trial fit of each wheel before mounting the tire; if there is a problem, it is better to know now and not after the tire has been mounted.

Place the custom wheel in the tire changer, using a piece of carpet to protect the underside (Fig. 6-11).

Insert the valve stem in the hole. Some rims require a special steel valve stem that bolts into place between rubber seals. This type is expensive, but is chrome-plated for looks and lasts longer than the conventional sort.

Coat the tire beads with rubber lubricant and force the tire over the rim as far as it will go by hand (Figs. 6-12 and 6-13). Now take the long bar and roll the tire bead onto the rim (Fig. 6-14). Use use a wet cloth between the tool and the rim to prevent scratches.

A word here about power-driven tire machines: If at all possible, use a hand-operated machine to protect the rim. Some power machines can be adjusted for minimum output. Shops

Fig. 6-11. The first step is to secure the rim on the tire-mounting machine. (Courtesy Customizing Center.)

Fig. 6-12. Coat the beads liberally with tire lubricant. (Courtesy Customizing Center.)

that charge extra to mount custom rims usually know their business and take special precautions—the extra dollar or two per rim is worth it.

Release the rim from the machine, but leave it on the platform. If you mounted the wheel upside down (as is normally done with pickup-truck rims), this is the time to turn it over.

Wrap a compression band around the tire and inflate the band to help seat the tire against the beads. (The band is not necessary for tube-type tires.) Now inflate the tire until the beads seat. Do not have your hands anywhere near the beads when inflating and never apply more than 45 psi to a

Fig. 6-13. Work the bead over the rim by hand as far as it will go. (Courtesy Customizing Center.)

light-truck or passenger-car tire. If more than 45 psi is required, stop and start over.

Now reduce tire pressure to the recommended value.

MOUNTING TUBE-TYPE TIRES

Only the largest truck tires require tubes as a matter of course, but I will cover tubed tires in case you have been

Fig. 6-14. Use the tire tool to roll the bead over the rim. It is a good idea to protect the rim with a wet cloth between it and the tool. (Courtesy Customizing Center.)

unlucky enough to purchase a porous rim. The mounting procedure is the same until you have one bead rolled over the rim and the upper bead outside of it. Inflate the tube slightly—just enough to take the wrinkles out of it—and sprinkle talcum powder on the tube and inside the tire. The danger with tube-type tires is that the tube can be damaged when the bead is rolled over the rim. If the tube is pinched between the tire and the rim, it will be torn. Talcum powder lubricates the tube so it will slide out of the way.

Slip the tube in place in the tire and gently push the valve stem through the hole in the rim. Examine the hole to make certain it is large enough to accept the stem. If the hole is too small, use a round, tapered file to enlarge it. Smooth off any burrs that would damage the tube or valve stem.

Now, very carefully roll the outer bead of the tire over the rim. Go slowly to avoid pinching the tube. When the bead is over the rim, rotate the tire so that valve stem stands straight and inflate the tire, supporting it as shown in Fig. 6-15. You won't have to bother with a compression band to seat the bead.

MOUNTING

Run the lug nuts or stud bolts up by hand, following the torque sequences shown in Fig. 6-16. Torque to manufacturer's recommendation and recheck several times during the first few hundred miles of operation.

Fig. 6-15. Inflate the tire. (Courtesy Customizing Center.)

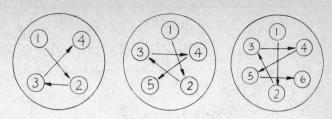

Fig. 6-16. Do not put an air wrench to a cast wheel; torque by hand in the appropriate sequence. Wheel manufacturers apply torque limits.Check the torque several times during the week after installation. (Courtesy Customizing Center.)

BALANCING

There are many ways to balance a wheel, ranging from a quick and easy static balance to the much more accurate and time-consuming dynamic method. The tire salesman will want you to balance the tires upon purchase. It is better to balance the tires after they have run 500-1000 miles, although this might cause logistics problems for the tire store.

Run the tires gently for the first 500 miles or so. Although tire salesmen disagree, tire engineers insist that a break-in period is needed. After break-in, have the tires balanced while they are still warm from the road. Hot balancing is especially important with nylon tires. The shop must cooperate and have the machine waiting as you drive up; if they balk at this service, find a shop that will provide it.

Custom wheels built-up from stock rims accept ordinary clip-on wheel weights. Cast aluminum wheels require stick-on weights.

While clearance should have been checked before, the real test is on the road. Steer for bumps, climb steep driveways, make tight turns, and examine the sidewalls and inner fenders for evidence of rubbing. Interference problems must be dealt with immediately. Sometimes the cure is as simple as bending the inner lip of the fender or as demanding as adding fender flares. Fortunately pickup trucks are forgiving and only the widest tires require body modifications.

Suppose the tires extend beyond the fenders? In most cases you can solve the difficulty with fender flares and flaps. However, some states limit the amount of flare offset. Wisconsin stipulates a 2-inch maximum; Nevada limits vehicle width to 102 inches; and both New Mexico and North Carolina have a 96-inch maximum width. Check with your state police.

Chapter 7

Safety First:

Mounting Fire Extinguishers

Most automotive fires are triggered by shorts in the electrical system. Others originate from oil or fuel spilled on the exhaust manifold. Leaking fuel lines and rocker cover gaskets are the major culprits. Occasionally an engine room will go up because of a faulty inlet needle in the carburetor.

Fire risk can be minimized by:

- Installing a fusible link in the positive battery cable. Links can be purchased from automotive-parts houses.
- Individually fusing each circuit.
- Keeping the engine compartment clean.
- Replacing flexible fuel and oil lines before they show obvious deterioration.
- Replacing rocker-cover gaskets upon the first evidence of leakage.
- Servicing fuel filters and renewing the carburetor inlet needle and seat at the first evidence of wear.

Electric fuel pumps are not appropriate for street machines. If you must run one, connect the hot lead in series with a pump-shutdown switch. This switch senses fuel pressure and opens the circuit should a leak develop.

But no vehicle is immune to fire, and you should carry a fire extinguisher.

A good, rechargable 2 1/2-pound fire extinguisher can be purchased for between $10 and $15. The price goes up a bit for

Fig. 7-1. Once the location is determined, the bracket is installed with sheet-metal screws.

a chromed cannister. Mount the fire extinguisher inside of the cab where it will be instantly accessible. Look for a cool, out-of-the-way spot where it won't be disturbed. You definitely don't want to position the extinguisher where someone's head would strike it in an accident. This rules out a door-pillar installation. The cab wall behind the seats, the floor alongside the seats, the passenger-side kick panels are good locations. The installation illustrated in Figs. 7-1 through 7-3 is on the floor, next to the driver's seat.

The bracket attaches with sheet-metal screws. Hold the bracket in place and check for clearance. Mark the floor for the holes, and check the underside of the cab for possible brake- or fuel-line interference. Do not attempt to drill through carpet; the cords will wrap themselves around the bit, marring the carpet. Instead make a small X-shaped cut in the

Fig. 7-2. Protect the nozzle with tape. Leave a large flap so the tape can be removed easily.

Fig. 7-3. The fire extinguisher should be shaded from the sun and recharged as necessary.

carpet, centered over each hole. Choose a drill bit that is slightly smaller than the root (or tooth-base) diameter. For example, a No. 8 screw requires a 9/64-inch bit; a No. 10 requires an 11/64 inch.

I recommend that you cover the nozzle with metallic tape to keep dirt out of the nozzle. (But don't forget to remove the tape in an emergency!)

Chapter 8

Two Easy Ones: Installing a Grille Guard and a Rear Bumper

Some of the most effective custom touches are bolt-on jobs, requiring no more than an hour from start to finish.

GRILLE GUARD

Grille guards are necessary for serious off-road work to protect the radiator from brush damage. Competitors also use them as brackets for additional lighting.

Competition grille guards are traditionally finished in matte black, but street versions are sometimes chrome-plated for glitter. The example illustrated here (Figs. 8-1 through 8-5) was designed by RVI for street or off-road use.

The grille guard, in addition to the protection it offers, is a handsome accessory for any pickup truck. Most grille guards are bolt-ons and easy to install. In some cases you do not have to drill holes in the bumper or frame for the manufacturers have cleverly taken advantage of existing bolts and holes. A grille guard can be installed in less than 15 minutes with a couple of wrenches.

A grille guard is a good place to start for the customizer who is just getting his feet wet.

REAR BUMPER

As delivered from the factory, a pickup is sans rear bumper, unless the customer pays extra. And even if the customer does pay, he receives a steel pressing, painted battleship gray. One sure way to give your pickup that custom

Fig. 8-1. This installation involves a bolt-together grille guard and the chrome plating flashed over some of the threads. The threads must be chased with a tap.

Fig. 8-2. The first step is to fit the sideplates to the bumper. Remove the carriage bolt already in the bumper and slip the sideplate into position. The frame attachment uses an existing bolt; remove the bolt, line up the holes, and replace the bolt. It's as simple as that.

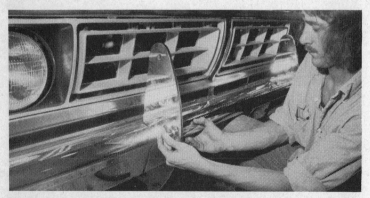

Fig. 8-3. With both sideplates bolted up, it's time to mount the crossbars. Leaving the sideplates a little loose will make things easier. Chrome-plated washers and bolts are supplied with the kit.

52

Fig. 8-4. Even the tabs for mounting auxiliary lights are provided.

Fig. 8-5. Completed installation with lights on the lower bar adds class to the F-100.

Fig. 8-6. There is no stock bumper (or a spare tire for that matter) but the license-plate bracket must be removed.

Fig. 8-7. Getting the bumper out of the box can be more difficult than installing it.

look is with a specialty bumper, complete with a trailer-hitch ball.

This is a simple customizing touch, a bolt-on that really makes the truck stand out. Plus it adds protection and safety. The bumper shown here is a Safe-Tee, constructed of chromed diamond platesteel. Installing the bumper takes only a few minutes, but it changes the appearance of the truck 100%.

The Safe-Tee is a quality item with all hardware supplied in the kit, even down to the license-plate lamps (Figs. 8-6 through 8-11). Since there is usually no stock bumper to

Fig. 8-8. The brackets hook over the frame and allow you to balance the bumper while helper inserts the bolts.

Fig. 8-9. Two bolts on each side support the bumper.

remove, one of the headaches is eliminated. However, getting the Safe-Tee bumper out of the box can be a problem—they really pack them well so none of that chrome gets scratched during shipping.

Fig. 8-10. Slip the license-plate lamps into place and splice the connections.

Fig. 8-11. The custom bumper really adds to the Ford.

The bumper, like the grille guard, uses existing bolts and brackets. There is nothing to weld, grind, or drill. The toughest part is balancing the bumper on your knee while a helper slides the bolts home.

Chapter 9

Sound Systems

There are several factors you want to consider before installing your sound system:

- How much room do you have?
- How sophisticated a system do you want?
- How many speakers will you need?
- Should you hide the system to prevent theft?

SELECTION

Stereo radio, tape decks, and CB radios should be chosen by the reputation of the manufacturer and on the basis of the testimony of your ears (Figs. 9-1 through 9-5). Listen to friends' systems and demonstration units in the stores before you make the final decision. Stereo systems, particularly those that give "living-room" sound quality, require a great deal of space, sometimes more space than is available in the cab. Check with the dealer.

INSTALLATION

In the way of tools you will need screwdrivers (Phillips and slotted), a razor knife, pliers, a wire stripper, a crimping tool, tin snips, a coping or keyhole saw, an electric drill motor and bits, vinyl electrical tape, and rubber grommets.

Fig. 9-1. A display of the sort you would find in an audio center. Try several systems before you buy; your ears are the best judge.

In-dash units are easiest to install and the most secure from theft (Figs. 9-6 and 9-7). Designed to replace the existing radio, once installed in-dash units are difficult and time-consuming to remove. The result is professional-looking when you use a faceplate and knobs that match the truck's interior. These parts are available from most stereo manufacturers.

Fig. 9-2. The Boman 40-channel CB is in combination with AM/FM stereo. This in-dash model looks factory-installed.

Fig. 9-3. An RCA in-dash CB/AM/FM/FM stereo with a faceplate designed to match truck interiors.

Fig. 9-4. Another RCA in-dash unit; this one with AM/FM/FM stereo and tape deck.

Fig. 9-5. An AM/FM/FM stereo receiver designed to replace the original-equipment receiver.

Under-dash units can be hung from the dash, hidden under the seat, in the glove box, mounted on the console, or, if space is at a premium, perched on the transmission tunnel. Whatever location you choose, make certain it can support the weight and, if a tape player is involved, will allow it to be mounted not more than 30° off the horizontal (Fig. 9-8). A greater tilt will affect the sound.

Of course, stereo requires at least two speakers. In a small-cab mini, two may be enough. In a larger full-size pickup, especially one that has thick layers of sound-absorbing carpeting and padding, you may prefer a four-speaker system (Fig. 9-9). For best sound, the front-door panels are considered the prime location. You may use either flush- or surface-mount speakers. The flush mount is the most appealing to the eye, unless the surface-mount speaker is styled. In addition to door panels, flush-mount speakers may be built into the kick panels behind the seats. When installed, only the cover, (usually a rubber-covered pad or grille) is visible (Figs. 9-10 through 9-15).

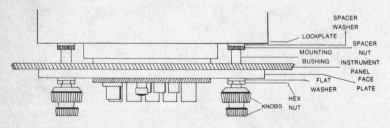

Fig. 9-6. An in-dash mounting arrangement, showing the use of bushings to position the knobs relative to the dash.

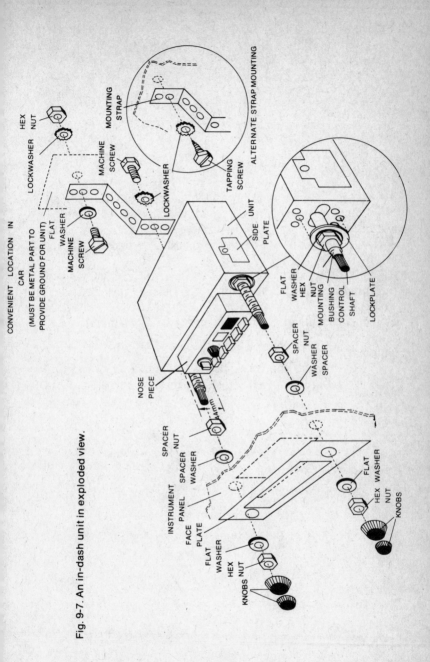

Fig. 9-7. An in-dash unit in exploded view.

CONVENIENT LOCATION IN CAR
(MUST BE METAL PART TO PROVIDE GROUND FOR UNIT)

HEX NUT
LOCKWASHER
FLAT WASHER
MACHINE SCREW

MACHINE SCREW
LOCKWASHER

MOUNTING STRAP
LOCKWASHER
TAPPING SCREW
ALTERNATE STRAP MOUNTING

MACHINE SCREW

SIDE PLATE
UNIT

FLAT WASHER
HEX NUT
MOUNTING BUSHING
CONTROL SHAFT
LOCKPLATE

NOSE PIECE

14mm

SPACER NUT
WASHER SPACER

SPACER NUT
SPACER WASHER

INSTRUMENT PANEL
FACE PLATE

FLAT WASHER
HEX NUT
KNOBS

FLAT WASHER
HEX NUT
KNOBS

61

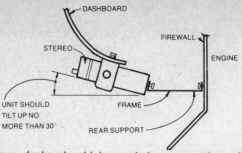

Fig. 9-8. Tape decks should be angled no more thean 30° from the horizontal.

Unless you go back many years, pickup trucks have 12-volt, negative-ground electrical systems for which stereo and CB units are designed. In-dash installation procedures are obvious, so I will confine this discussion to under-dash and mount installation.

Place the stereo or CB in its bracket and try several mounting locations. Check for gear-selector, glove-box door, and ashtray clearance. Once you're satisfied that the component is in an acceptable position, mark the fastener holes. Check the underside of the panel for electric wiring or plumbing.

Center punch the holes before drilling to keep the drill from "dancing." If you are drilling through carpet, make a

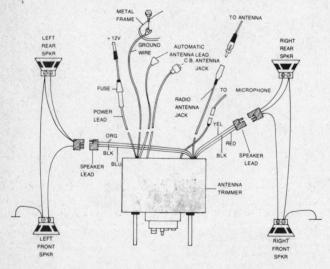

Fig. 9-9. A typical four-speaker hookup.

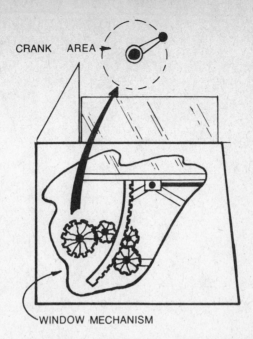

CRANK AREA

WINDOW MECHANISM

Fig. 9-10. Check window and window-crank operation before installing the speaker.

Fig. 9-11. Trim the door panel to accept the speaker.

Fig. 9-12. Using the cover as a template, mark the mounting holes.

small X cut with a razor knife before attempting to drill. Otherwise the bit will snare the carpet, unraveling it.

Drill the center hole for the bracket first (Fig. 9-16). Then you can hang the bracket and drill the remaining holes using it as a template. Don't forget the lock washers. Otherwise, vibration (even through you may not feel it) will soon shake fasteners loose. Attach the unit to the bracket. Most CBs are secured with large thumbscrews for portability. (Nobody

Fig. 9-13. Drill out the holes.

Fig. 9-14. Connect the speaker wires.

Fig. 9-15. The finished job looks like original equipment.

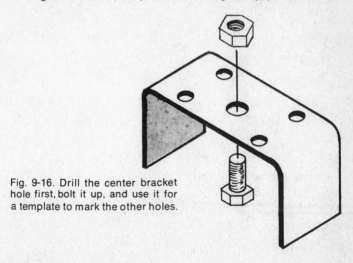

Fig. 9-16. Drill the center bracket hole first, bolt it up, and use it for a template to mark the other holes.

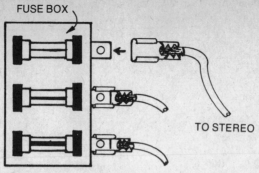

FUSE BOX

TO STEREO

Fig. 9-17. The best source of power is an unused terminal at the fuse block.

leaves an under-dash in place in an unattended vehicle.) You might want to use a slide-in bracket in which the electrical connections are made when the unit is slipped into place. Both are installed in the same manner.

Most kits include a strip of perforated metal for support at the rear of the unit. Attach one end of this backing strip to the stereo or CB and the other end to the firewall or a dashboard brace. The unit should be mounted solidly.

Now it's time to connect the wiring. In most cases the wires are connected to a quick-release plug so the stereo or CB can be easily removed. Find a hot lead at the fuse block that is located under the dash or on the cab side of the firewall (Fig. 9-17). You will want a continuously hot wire, one that is not

Fig. 9-18. Wire strippers are not necessary, but speed the work.

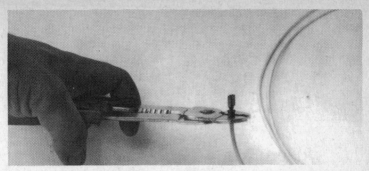

Fig. 9-19. Solderless connectors are crimped with a special tool.

controlled by the ignition switch for tape-deck power. Should the tape player stop with the tape still in place, the pinch roller can be damaged. A CB can be wired to the accessory side of the switch. If there are no available hot terminals at the fuse box, you will have to splice into a hot line from somewhere else. The cigar-lighter lead is a good choice, since the circuit is noncritical and the lead is easily accessible.

For best results, use solderless connectors (Figs. 9-18 through 9-20). Merely twisting the wires around each other is an invitation to trouble.

Connect the ground wire next. One end attaches to the unit through the plug and the other attaches to metal at the dash or floor. Before securing the ground wire, scrape paint off the area where the wire makes contact.

Run the leads from the speaker to the unit. In the case of a CB, this will not be necessary, unless you mount an additional speaker or under-hood PA speaker. Protect the fragile wires by routing them under the doorsill scuff plates or along the transmission hump. Use grommets wherever the wires pass through drilled holes.

Fig. 9-20. The finished connection is stronger than it would be if soldered.

Chapter 10
Custom Carpet

Most trucks come from the factory with a plain-looking rubber mat. This may be great for commercial or off-road use, but for a street truck, that mat has to be replaced with carpet.

In addition to the visual appeal carpet adds, it acts as sound and heat insulation. All the better to hear the stereo, my dear.

What type of carpet is best? It depends on the use. For the truck that will see double duty as both a utility vehicle and as a showpiece, indoor/outdoor carpet is the best bet. Indoor/outdoor is durable and washable. Some customizers balk at indoor/outdoor carpeting because it is not as attractive as high/low shag or even original-equipment carpet. But you can't have everything.

One of the most popular choices is high/low shag in multicolors to match the interior and exterior trim of the pickup. Made of tough nylon, this carpet can withstand some harsh use, although not as much as, say, indoor/outdoor carpet. High/low shag has one other attraction: It hides mistakes. It can be patched—without showing marks of the surgery. This is a very helpful quality when a careless friend burns a hole with a cigarette or climbs in your pickup with dirty shoes. Shag can also be used on kick panels, the back wall of the cab, and on the doors.

The third choice is the small-loop carpet of the type used in luxury automobiles. The material can be had as an option on some trucks; unfortunately, the factory installation leaves a great deal to be desired. In most cases the weave is thin and wears quickly. Nor is truck carpet anchored as it is in passenger cars. If you use OEM carpet, make sure you secure it with carpet adhesive.

Whatever the material you choose, the technique of installation is the same.

To install new carpet, remove the rubber mat but don't throw it away yet. Clean the areas to be carpeted. It is best to remove the seats and anything else (some pickups have the spare mounted in the cab) that could get in the way (Fig. 10-1). Using the rubber mat as a pattern, cut the carpet to fit. Leave a little extra around all the edges as margin for error.

Start at the back of the cab and work forward. Have a can of adhesive (3M Fast Tack is popular with customizers) and a brush ready and work with a small area until the carpet lies flat and neat (Figs. 10-2 and 10-3). This is easy until you get to the areas under the dashboard where you have to go around the brake and throttle pedals (Fig. 10-4). Here the trick is to slit the carpet and then glue it down behind the obstruction (Figs. 10-5 and 10-6). If you are careful with the adhesive, the slit will never show.

Another problem area is the driveline tunnel—you will find that the carpet won't conform to the shape. Cut out small pie-shaped pieces of carpet where it bulges and then glue the edges down. Nobody will be able to tell.

Fig. 10-1. Remove the seats and other encumbrances and scrub the floor.

Fig. 10-2. Wet a small area of the floor with adhesive.

The kick panels (forward of the door and under the dash) are easy. Either remove the kick panel (it is secured by Phillips screws and spring clips) and glue the carpet to it, or if you prefer, carpet the panel while it is in place (Figs. 10-7 and 10-8).

A nice touch is to carpet the lower part of the door panels for protection against scuff damage. Cut and trim the carpet to

Fig. 10-3. Roll out the trimmed carpet, smoothing the wrinkles with your knees.

Fig. 10-4. Start at the rear of the cab and work to the front, stretching the carpet as you lay it.

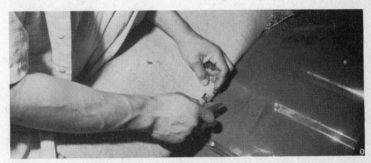

Fig. 10-5. Slit the carpet to fit over obstructions.

Fig. 10-6. The under-dash area can be difficult, especially on the driver's side. Careful trimming and fitting can give excellent results—the carpet will look as if it grew in place.

Fig. 10-7. Here a kick panel is being carpeted. The shag blends in with the floor without a noticeable seam.

Fig. 10-8. A little attention to detail will really set off the carpet job. A dab of adhesive on the edges of the kick panel will keep the shag standing proud.

Fig. 10-9. The F-100 is a natural for scuff pads under the doors.

Fig. 10-10. Once the adhesive is applied, the carpet is pressed into place.

fit a natural contour of the door or the door panel and glue it in place (Figs. 10-9 and 10-10). For the full treatment you might want to carpet the back wall of the cab from the floor to the rear window (Fig. 10-11). Some customizers carpet the headliner. I don't go along with the idea, though, since the carpet collects dust and releases it every time you hit a bump.

Fig. 10-11. The result is fantastic.

Chapter 11

Sidepipes

Stock exhaust plumbing can hamper ground clearance and, to one degree or another, strangle the engine in its own exhaust fumes. A properly designed after-market exhaust system aids performance and fuel economy by reducing back pressure. From the point of view of looks, the best choice among after-market systems is a set of sidepipes.

Sidepipes are also known as "lake pipes" because they are reminiscent of the exhaust plumbing on Bonneville and El Mirage cars some years back. These cars were fitted with large-diameter pipes running down each side of the chassis terminating ahead of the rear wheels. The pipes were connected in parallel with the stock exhaust system and were capped for street use.

Modern sidepipes replace the original exhaust system, after the model of racing Corvettes of the 1960s. The pipes are large in diameter and may be given a more massive appearance by heat shields. The mufflers are integral with the pipes and are generally lined with fiberglass to dampen high-frequency sounds. The result is a cheerful burble that becomes a growl as the throttle plates are opened.

MOUNTING

The first step is to remove the constipated stock exhaust system (Fig. 11-1). It is amazing how quickly rust and corrosion build up, so count on using a torch to remove the

Fig. 11-1. The Chevy LUV exhaust system. It gets the job done, but leaves much to be desired in terms of performance and looks.

stock plumbing (Fig. 11-2). Don't neglect to wear safety goggles; flecks of rust can do serious eye damage.

Now position the brackets that will secure the sidepipes and bolt them into place between rubber bushings (Figs. 11-3 and 11-4). If the brackets are not isolated in rubber, the system will shake, rattle, and ultimately self-destruct. Hold the sidepipe up in position and mark where the pipe will touch the body panels.

Gain the necessary clearance with a ball-peen hammer (Fig. 11-5). Since these body mods are on the underside of the vehicle, they will not be seen; but it's a good idea to protect the paint with masking tape. With everything all set, weld the sidepipe to the brackets. Repeat the procedure for the

Fig. 11-2. Muffler clamps can be rusted solid—a torch is helpful.

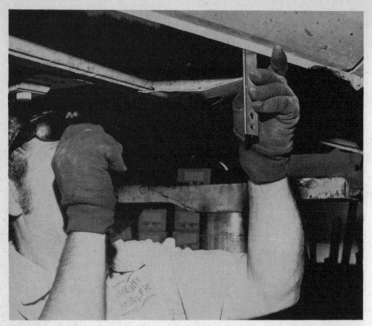

Fig. 11-3. Position the brackets that will hold the sidepipes in place.

remaining pipe. If it's only looks that you want, you can stop here and many customizers do just that. We've seen trucks with dummy sidepipes (at least the rear wheels stay clean).

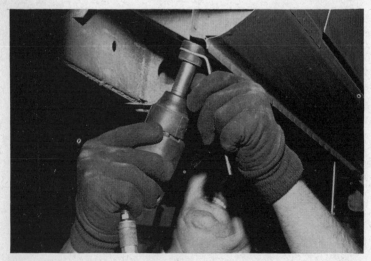

Fig. 11-4. Secure the brackets with rubber bushings to reduce vibration and noise.

Fig. 11-5. Hold the sidepipe in position to determine if the sheet metal must be dinged out of the way. Usually just the lip at the underside of the body interfers. Protecting the paint with masking tape would be a good idea.

Fig. 11-6. Now the inside of the sidepipe is welded to the brackets. Note the special muffler stand to hold the pipe in place.

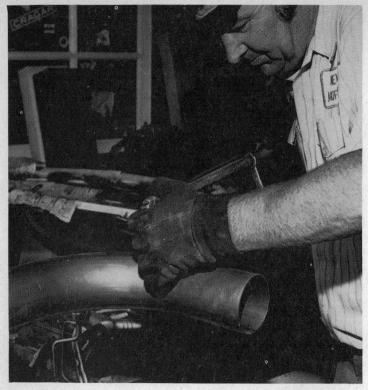

Fig. 11-7. Here is where experience helps—the large pipe must be cut to mate with the smaller pipe.

CONNECTING

It's really best to have an expert do the next part, but you should know what he is going to do, even if you don't try it yourself.

Here is where experience and welding skill pay off—the 4-inch sidepipes must be mated to the 2-inch exhaust pipe by means of a stepdown. The larger pipe is cut to length and the stepdown pipe is welded to the end (Figs. 11-7 through 11-10). Now things really get complicated.

A balance tube—a length of exhaust tubing connecting both sides of the system—helps equalize the exhaust impulses and modulates the tone. It eliminates that goat-like bllaa-blat sound on acceleration and popback during coastdown. But installation requires some skill with the torch (Figs. 11-11 through 11-13).

A coat of flat black finishes the job (Fig. 11-14).

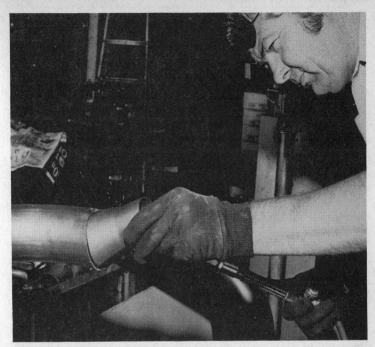

Fig. 11-8. The stepdown pipe is welded at the correct angle.

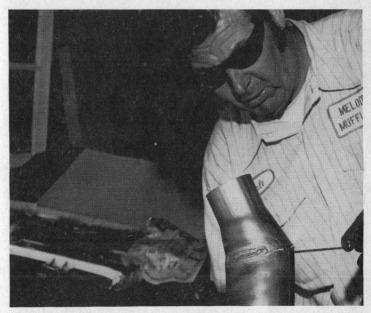

Fig. 11-9. The weld is run all the way around to prevent exhaust leaks.

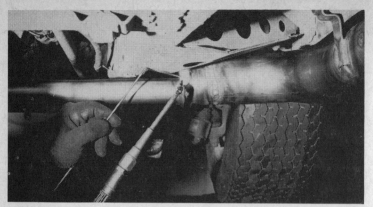

Fig. 11-10. Welding the exhaust pipe to the stepdown pipe completes the initial stage of installation. Note how the bracket has been bent to hold the sidepipe.

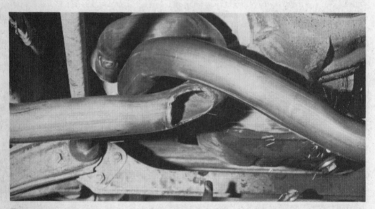

Fig. 11-11. What appears to be a terrible hole in the exhaust pipe is the start of the balance-tube installation. Ragged hole was made with the torch.

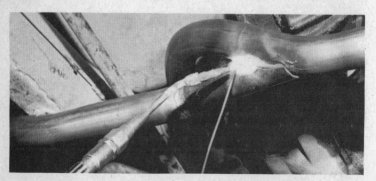

Fig. 11-12. The balance tube is positioned and welded.

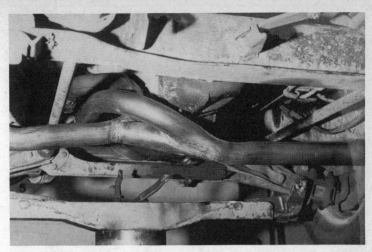

Fig. 11-13. The balance tube equalizes the pressure between the exhaust pipes before the exhaust gases get to the mufflers. Without a balance tube the sound would be like two buzzing lawnmowers; with the balance tube you get a deep, throaty rumble.

Fig. 11-14. A careful application of heat-resistant paint will keep this set of pipes looking good for years to come.

Chapter 12

Step Sides Are Back

Nostalgia is big—even Detroit has reissued step-side beds for their current pickups. But what about the mini-trucks? Are owners of small trucks stuck with utilitarian beds that haul plenty of cargo, but look square and boxy? Not any more. Now you can install an after-market step-side bed (Fig. 12-1).

California Step Side Manufacturing makes stepside kits that are marketed through auto specialty shops. The kit consists of a heavy-gauge steel box, two fiberglass fenders, taillights, and all necessary hardware. The bed is primed and the fiberglass fenders are covered in white gel: Both ready to be color-coated to match your truck's paint.

The first order of business is to get the old box off the truck (Fig. 12-2). Gather a few friends to help with the lifting. The bed is attached with six to eight bolts (depending upon the make of truck) that are removed with a socket and ratchet handle. The bed rides on rubber mounting pads that are retained for the new step-side bed.

Next, disconnect the wiring for the taillights and license-plate light at the terminals; the wiring will be reconnected later. You must remove the vapor tank and rubber lines at the fuel tank on the Ford Courier; the lines will be reinstalled after the new bed is in place (Fig. 12-3). Once the bolts are removed, bring your friends into play to lift the old bed off the chassis—just lift it up and walk to the rear. Perhaps you can sell the old bed to a body shop or a trailer manufacturer. You could always turn it into a planter in the backyard.

Fig. 12-1. Installing a step-side bed is an effective way to give that nostalgic look to your mini.

Fig. 12-2. The stock bed lifts off its mounting pads once the wiring, fuel lines, and the attaching bolts are removed.

California Step Side makes one bed for all minis; only the hardware is different. On some trucks a bracket must be attached to the frame to support the "steps" that will be added later. Now you walk the new bed into place and position it

Fig. 12-3. Plug the fuel lines and lash the loose hardware out of the way until the new bed is installed.

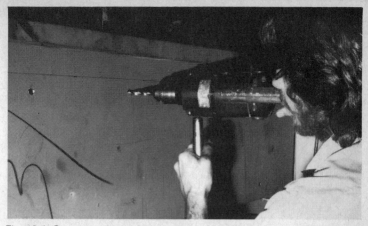

Fig. 12-4. Once you determine the correct fender location, drill bolt holes in the bed.

correctly. Get under the truck and have your friends move the bed until the bolt holes line up. Start all the bolts before tightening any of them. Then tighten from the center bolts to the outside.

Next, bolt the fenders in place. This also requires the help of a friend. Hold the fenders in place and mark the bed and the fenders for the mounting bolts. Drill the fenders, recheck the mounting position, and drill the bed—it's that easy (Figs. 12-4 and 12-5).

Fig. 12-5. Now secure the fenders.

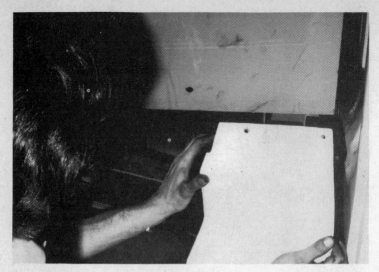

Fig. 12-6. The steps (constructed of fiberglass) are fitted after the bed is mounted and adjusted.

The steps bolt directly to the fenders, but (in this example) are supported from the underside with the brackets installed earlier (Figs. 12-6 through 12-8). The brackets make the steps functional, since they will support a man's weight. Steps mean easier loading and unloading. The major work is over—you can dismiss your friends (if they haven't left already to start

Fig. 12-7. The bolts for the steps pass through the bed and chassis for strength.

Fig. 12-8. The steps are mounted to the fenders at two points.

on their own mini-truck conversions) and attend to details such as connecting the lights and fuel lines.

The light brackets are installed (see Fig. 12-9) by drilling the pillars at the rear of the bed to accept the bracket bolts.

Fig. 12-9. Lighting brackets are installed on the outside-rear channel of the box for a neat, simple installation.

Fig. 12-10. This Courier looks good, even though the bed has not yet been painted.

Fig. 12-11. A little paint and alloy wheels work wonders. The Courier has been transformed from an ugly duckling into full-blown swan.

Fig. 12-12. California Step Side beds fit most minis. Here is a Toyota installation.

Fig. 12-13. The addition of a step-side bed gives the custom painter more to work with. He now has flowing lines and curves, rather than a slab-side box to paint.

Reinstall the license plate and you are ready for the road. The bed won't carry as much now, but it certainly makes the truck look better (Figs. 12-10 through 12-14).

Fig. 12-14. This Datsun 620 pickup got the full treatment. Note the flared rear fenders and the custom grille. Minis can look great!

Chapter 13
Sunroofs

A few years ago a sunroof was an expensive, hard-to-install accessory with complex hardware that never seemed to work right. The advent of the pop-up type sunroof has changed all that (Fig. 13-1). Today sunroofs are almost as popular as mag wheels, and almost as easy to mount (Fig. 13-2).

Not only does a sunroof look good, it also provides an additional vent for the cab. As you learned in high school

Fig. 13-1. This photo illustrates the two-piece construction typically used.

physics, hot air rises. If it has a place to escape, then the cab will be cooler and you will not have to run the air conditioner as much.

Installing a sunroof is not difficult, provided you have a few tools, including a saber saw, tin snips, screwdriver, drill

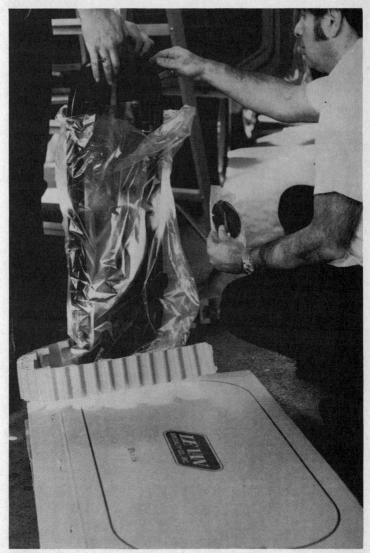

Fig. 13-2. The sunroof is packaged in plastic to prevent scratches. Note the template provided on the box—don't destroy the box since you'll need the template when cutting the roof.

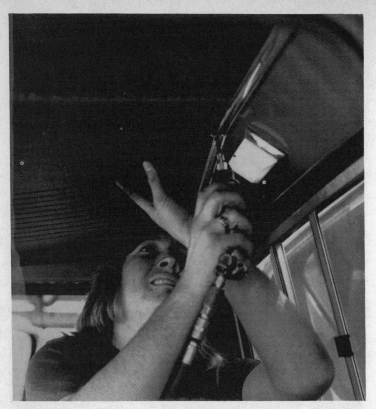

Fig. 13-3. The headliner must be removed.

Fig. 13-4. The wires running along the center roof brace have to be routed to the side of the sunroof. A good pair of metal snips helps when removing the center brace.

Fig. 13-5. If the welds at the front are stubborn, work the brace up and down until the metal fatigues and finally breaks off. Trim sharp edges that would wear through the headliner.

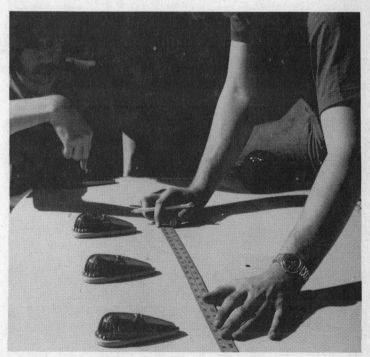

Fig. 13-6. Now it's time to measure to be certain the sunroof will be centered. This pickup is already equipped with rooftop running lights.

Fig. 13-7. Measure the back of the roof panel as well. Not only must the sunroof be centered, it must be aligned from front to rear.

motor, and bits. Take your time with the job, and you will not be bothered with leaks or embarrassed by misalignment.

First you will have to remove the headliner and (on some models) the center roof brace (Figs. 13-3 through 13-5). Then, using the pattern supplied on the box as a guide, scribe the cutout on the roof (Figs. 13-6 through 13-8). Unless you have a

Fig. 13-8. Align the template with the marks previously made.

Fig. 13-9. Once the pattern is marked, drill a pilot hole. The hole gives you a place to start the saw blade.

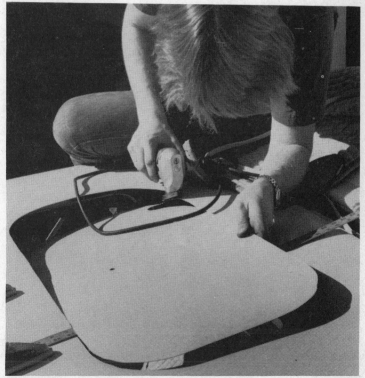

Fig. 13-10. The moment of truth. Carefully follow the outline with a saber saw.

Fig. 13-11. Have a friend support the cutout from the inside. Here the assistant uses a length of wood to keep the metal from falling into the interior.

well thought-out alternative in mind, center the cutout on the roof panel, with its trailing edge square with the back of the panel. Once you are satisfied that the cutout is symmetrically located, drill a pilot hole for the saber saw (Fig. 13-9). Have an assistant hold the section up from the inside so the freshly-cut metal does not fall and tear the seats (Figs. 13-10 and 13-11). Trim the headliner to match the hole (Fig. 13-12).

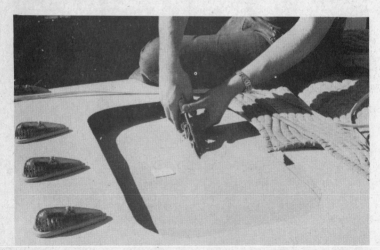

Fig. 13-12. After the metal is removed, the headliner must be trimmed to fit the hole. Have your assistant hold the headliner in place and cut using the hole as the pattern. Be careful not to tear the fabric.

Fig. 13-13. Install putty tape around the edge of the sunroof to prevent water leaks.

Place putty tape around the sealing edge of the sunroof (Fig. 13-13). Install the sunroof, reinstall the headliner, and secure the sunroof with the retainer and trim rings (Figs. 13-14 and 13-15).

Fig. 13-14. Slip the sunroof into place, checking that all edges are sealed with putty. Trim the excess with a razor knife and wipe the area with a damp rag.

Fig. 13-15. Slip the lower retainer ring into place and secure with the screws supplied in the kit. If the aluminum distorts, use a hammer and a small block of wood to bend it back into shape.

Finally, force the inside retaining ring into place with a hammer and block of wood. Hammering directly on the aluminum ring will dent and mar the surface.

Chapter 14
High Riders

Oversized tires can interfere with the fenders on a mini-truck. One way around this problem is to cut and reshape the fenders, adding flares as needed. The other way is to take advantage of the four-wheel-drive look and raise the body for clearance (Fig. 14-1).

Several high-rider kits are currently marketed to give mini-trucks the requisite altitude. For the most part these kits

Fig. 14-1. Once you have installed a high-rider kit, you can mount huge off-road tires for go-anywhere capability.

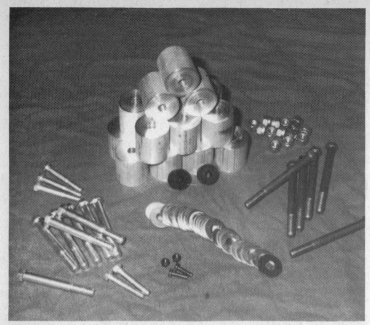

Fig. 14-2. The high-rider kit is complete and ready to install under your mini.

Fig. 14-3. The first step in the changeover is to remove the grille. It comes out easily.

use quality parts and get the job done, varying only in price— from semi- to super-expensive.

I recently watched Pat Marine, head wrench at Coast Datsun (Long Beach, Calif.), install a high-rise kit. This particular kit is intended for 1972 1/2-and-later Datsun 610s. Kit cost is something less than $100.

After unpacking and sorting the components, which consist of 17 metal spacers, 21 bolts, and a handful of nuts and washers (Fig. 14-2), Pat disconnected the "hot," or positive, cable at the battery.

CAB

The preliminary steps involve removing the grille, radiator, and front bumper (Figs. 14-3 and 14-4). The grille is removed to provide accessibility; however, modifications

Fig. 14-4. Next, the front bumper brackets must be removed.

Fig. 14-5. While the radiator remains undisturbed on the truck's frame, the position on the body will be different. Use a pair of pliers to bend the old mounting tabs out of the way.

Fig. 14-6. Two inches must be trimmed from the lower radiator hose.

must be made to the bumper and radiator mounts to accommodate the additional height (Fig. 14-5). The lower radiator hose on '75 and '76 models must be trimmed 2 inches to clear the fan and alternator brackets (Fig. 14-6).

Next, the seat-belt inertia reel (if present) and the bolts connecting the steering-column yoke to the dash are removed (Fig. 14-7). The final step before raising the cab is removing the nuts that hold the cab to the chassis (located on the underside of the truck). The bolts remain in place until the cab is raised.

The cab should be raised one side at a time with a jack placed under the outboard edge of the cab, about midway between the door pillars. The cab should be raised about 3 inches. Remove the original bolts, insert the longer bolts provided in the kit, and place steel spacers between the body and the original rubber spacers (Figs. 14-8 and 14-9). Once these steps have been completed, lower the body and install the rubber spacers, retaining washers, and nuts. The kit instructions call for switching the original middle and rear spacers. The nuts should be cinched until the rubber begins to

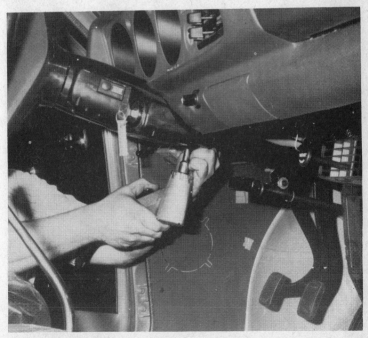

Fig. 14-7. The steering column must be loosened. Once everything is back in place, make absolutely certain that the steering column is secured.

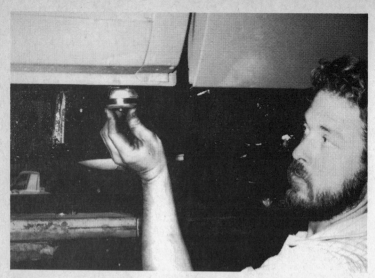

Fig. 14-8. Note the difference between the original position shown here and the new mount in the next illustration.

Fig. 14-9. This is what the completed installation of the pad, spacer, and new bolt should look like. Don't overtighten the bolt and damage the rubber mounting pad. Tighten just enough to bulge the pad.

bulge. The middle spacer is thick, leaving only a few threads exposed on the bolt. Tighten the nut so that its whole length is engaged on the threads for safety. Repeat these procedures on the other side of the cab.

BED

The bed receives much the same treatment as the cab, with one side secured before going to the other. The jack should be placed under the outboard edge of the bed at its balance point. Raise the bed 3 inches. It's a good idea to use a crowbar to separate the bed from the frame before jacking, since the two may not part easily.

Once the eight bed spacers are in place, realign the bed with the cab (Fig. 14-10). The sides of the cab and bed should be flush with a 3/4-inch gap between them. Tighten the nuts securely.

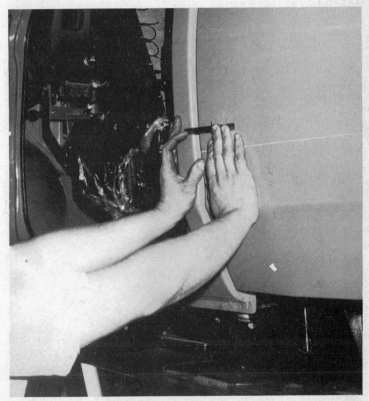

Fig. 14-10. Once the cab and pickup bed have been raised, they must be aligned. There should be 3/4 in. between the cab and the pickup bed.

FRONT BUMPER

Kit instructions call for cutting the left front-bumper bracket at its end hole to clear the steering box. For additional strength Pat recommends cutting the bracket at an angle behind the hole to make clearance without sacrificing bracket security (Fig. 14-11). An additional bolt is required which you'll have to supply. A handful of washers and an 8 × 60 mm bolt will do the job nicely. The bumper is raised with the aid of four spacers.

RADIATOR

As mentioned earlier, the radiator on this particular vehicle is secured to the body with a pair of tabs. Since the radiator will be mounted lower, these tabs should be bent out of the way. You will find two small holes 1 1/2 inches under the original mounting holes. Ream these holes to accept the bolts supplied in the kit. Attach the hoses and fill the radiator with coolant.

REAR BUMPER AND MISCELLANEOUS PARTS

If a rear bumper is to be installed, you will have to drill four mounting holes 2 inches under the original holes to compensate for the increased bed height. Connect the inertia

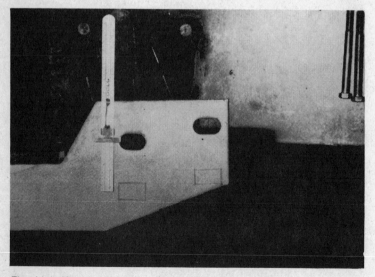

Fig. 14-1. New location for the bumper mounting holes. Location is 2 inches (center-to-center) below the stock mounting holes.

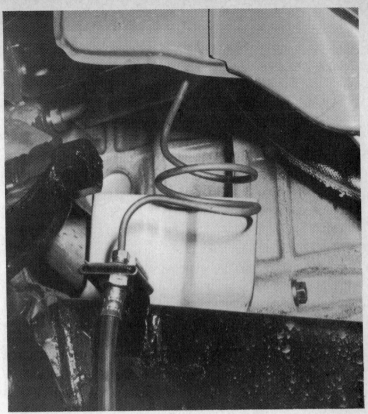

Fig. 14-12. Don't overlook the brake lines either. Simply expand the flex-absorption coils.

reels behind the seat in the cab and secure the steering-column yoke, using the two rubber spacers provided in the kit. Following this, check all hoses, cables, and wires for binding and clearance (Fig. 4-12). Connect the battery cable and you're ready to roll!

An experienced crew can install the kit in four hours. At home, without the aid of power tools, the project will require more time.

Chapter 15

Off-Road Racing

In the last few years mini-pickups have been dramatically successful in off-road racing, so successful that the mini is considered the way to go in two-wheel-drive classes. Some of the technology that fuels these race winners has filtered down to the street.

Jim Conner builds and drives one of the hottest Datsuns in California. He has piloted his 620 to victory in scores of events, including the Baja 500. While few street rodders would want a replica of Jim's Datsun, many of the ideas shown in the accompanying photos have real utility and will give your truck that *muy macho* off-road look (Figs. 15-1 through 15-27).

Some of these modifications are relatively simple to make; others require the services of a skilled welder. Individual parts—strengthened steering components, shock-mounting kits, skid pans, and the like—are available from Jim Conner Mini-Trucks in Glendale, Calif.

Fig. 15-1. Jim Conner's Datsun 620.

Fig. 15-2. No cargo here, the bed is pure practicality. Huge spare tire and rim are mounted aft for accessibility.

Fig. 15-3. Jim Conner in his "office." Note the padded shoulder by upholstery ace Al Taylor.

Fig. 15-4. Chronometers mounted on the inside of the passenger door are as important as any of the dash instruments. Door panel is made of light-gauge aluminum.

Fig. 15-5. The hood is finished in flat black. Note the pushbar from the House of Steel and the snap-on light covers from Al Taylor.

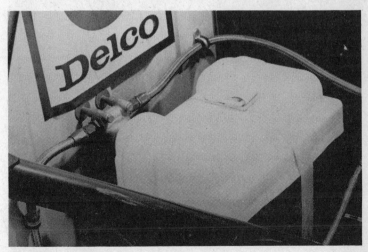

Fig. 15-6. The battery lives in the bed, inside a marine battery box. In the event of a rollover, the acid will be confined to the box.

Fig. 15-7.The lug wrench is clipped to the spare with bungee cord for instant access. Note the way a handle has been welded to the hold-down nut.

Fig. 15-8. A hydraulic bumper jack is anchored forward of the tire. Every tool and replacement part is stored for convenient, quick use.

Fig. 15-9. A Stewart-Warner pump supplies the gasoline through steel-braided AN lines. Attention to detail has made Conner's trucks dependable winners.

Fig. 15-10. Driver comfort is important during long, bone-jarring races. Iced Gatorade in the jug is fed through tubing to the driver and co-driver.

Fig. 15-11. K.C. Daylighters are mounted on rubber to protect the filaments from vibration. Conner routes the wiring in BX for security.

Fig. 15-12. Sheer power is less important than dependability. Silicon ignition cables and heat shields under the Solex carburetors show concern for desert temperatures.

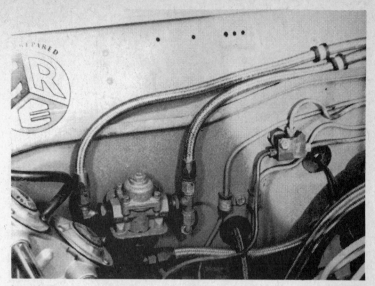

Fig. 15-13. A Stewart-Warner fuel regulation is used to limit the pressure to the carbs.

Fig. 15-14. The 610 carries a second coil and resistor mounted and ready to go should the first fail. Note the duct tape securing the master cylinder caps.

Fig. 15-15. Keeping the dust out of the engine is very important in off-road racing; Conner depends on washable-element Filtrons.

Fig. 15-16. Cross braces are added to the chassis; paired Gabriel Striders snub the suspension. Steel cables wrapped around the rear axle prevent damage when the truck becomes airborne.

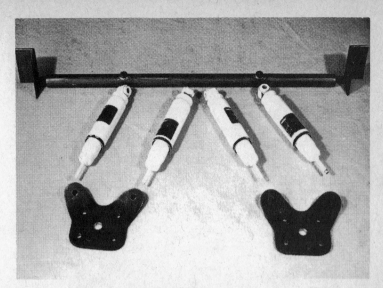

Fig. 15-17. Conner designed and builds the suspension package. Parts shown are for mounting the four-shock system over the rear axle.

Fig. 15-18. Up front it's the same story—make it bulletproof. Suspension components are reworked and dual shocks are added.

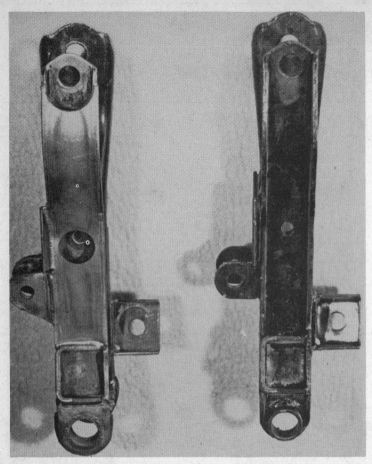

Fig. 15-19. Stock lower transverse arm (right) is boxed and welded. All mounting tabs and flanges are reinforced.

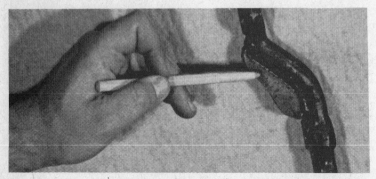

Fig. 15-20. A metal brace is added to the idler arm.

Fig. 15-21. The upper suspension arms are boxed and reinforced. In more than 5000 racing miles, Conner has yet to experience an A-arm failure.

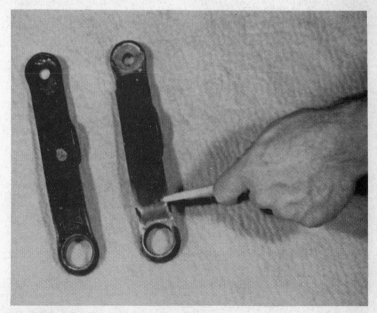

Fig. 15-22. Details, details. Even the oft-forgotten steering links get the toughening treatment.

Fig. 15-23. Dual shocks are used in the front. A heavy-duty, nonadjustable Garbiel is fitted in the stock position with a NASCAR-type Gabriel bringing up the rear.

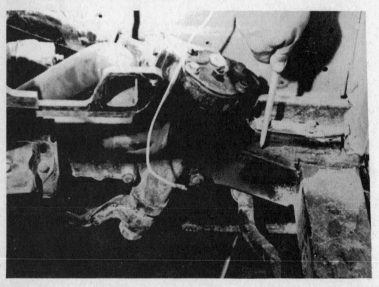

Fig. 15-24. Conner rewelds all factory welds and braces the weak spots.

Fig. 15-25. A set of horns may be your only means of communication with the pit crew. Conner's Datsun sounds like tractor-trailer rig with these air horns.

Fig. 15-26. Conner swears by Tacoma wheels; he once drove 50 miles on the rim to reach the next checkpoint.

Fig. 15-27. Standard equipment for off-road adventures is a husky skid plate to protect the soft undersides of the truck. From the looks of this plate, it's been doing its job.

Chapter 16

Four-Wheel Drive

There was a time when the four-wheel drive pickup was used only by farmers, hunters, game wardens, and construction workers. But those times are over. Today city streets and the driveways of suburbia are filled with high-riding, 4WD pickup trucks. In some instances, two-wheel drive trucks are modified for the 4WD look.

What is the four-wheel drive look? It's a high-stepping truck riding on the largest tires that can be shoehorned under the fenders. And these tires carry the howlingest, most aggressive tread patterns known to man. A rollbar—looking as if it had been made from Alaskan pipeline leftovers—looms over the bed, supporting quartz-iodide lamps with enough candlepower to blister paint. A grille guard and pushbar combination rides ahead of the front bumper for protection and intimidation. The crowning touch is a winch, geared to pull down small buildings.

In short, the four-wheel look is tough, beefy, macho, huge, bulletproof, go-anywhere, do-anything, last-forever. But it's not all cosmetics; the 4WD look is the expression of function (Fig. 16-1).

TIRES

Let's start with the tires. They are big and equipped with mud-throwing tread patterns because they need to be for off-road travel. Large, wide tires give better flotation in sand and mud, and are less likely to dig in and bury the truck. Aggressive tread lugs generate traction in mud, loose gravel,

Fig. 16-1. There is nothing like four-wheel drive for blasting through rough country.

snow, and (with reduced tire pressures) sand. These tires howl on the pavement—something very macho for owners into that sort of thing.

These monster tires have created a new series: LT tires. The most popular sizes are 10-15LT, 12-15LT, and now the even larger 14/32-15LT. Tires are purchased in matched sets. With a four-wheel drive vehicle, it is important that all four tires be the same size; otherwise, the transfer case and the differentials could be damaged. In, say, the 14/32-15LT size, the breakdown works like this: 14 means that the tire measures 14 inches across the section (the tread is slightly narrower), 32 indicates the rolling diameter (the most important measurement for 4WD), and 15 indicates the wheel diameter. The initials LT mean light-truck service. Several manufacturers supply LT tires and Goodrich has recently introduced an off-road radial—the first of its kind.

WHEELS

The stock steel wheel is pretty tough. A steel rim will bend if it hits an obstruction, but will usually hold air. The trouble with stock wheels is that they are too narrow for effective four-wheeling. The next step up is a wider rim; the wheel looks like the original, but accepts a wider tire. Most stock rims are 6 to 7 inches wide; custom steel rims measure from 8 to 12 inches. Refer to the chapter on tires for explanation of the relationship between tire size and rim width.

The spoked wheel with a steel hub and rim is popular with the four-wheel drive set. These wheels combine the style of custom wheels with the strength of steel. The third choice is an all-aluminum wheel, similar to those used on street machines. Aluminum wheels are strong in terms of load-carrying ability, but are susceptible to chipping in rugged terrain. If the chip comes out of the wrong place, such as the bead, then the tire will no longer hold air.

Race drivers are about evenly divided on this subject: Some prefer aluminum for light weight and load strength, others run steel for malleability.

ROLLBARS

Monster rollbars were also developed for practical reasons. A truck traversing the side of a mountain has some likelihood of ending up on its top. The drivers knew that a rollbar could prevent injury to the occupants—if not the vehicle—should a rollover occur. Since a truck is much heavier than a racing car, it was quickly learned that a massive rollbar was needed.

AXLE TRUSS

The truss is made of steel strap, welded or bolted to the ends and the center of the front axle assembly. It prevents the axle housing from flexing under a load or when hitting the sort of obstacles encountered in off-road driving. Without a truss, the factory welds would last about as long as a sardine at a barracuda convention.

SKID PLATE

The skid plate is usually constructed of steel (expensive racing versions may be fabricated from magnesium). It protects the vital parts of the vehicle from rocks and logs on the trail. Most owners mount one or more skid plates under the oil pan, front differential, transfer case (unless it is carried high, Ford fashion), drive shafts, fuel tanks, exhaust system, and rear differential. Ideally, a four-wheeler would like to armor the entire undercarriage of his vehicle—unfortunately, that isn't always possible.

LIGHTS

What about those lights mounted on the rollbar and front push bar? They are for real. Ordinary headlamps are almost useless for high-speed, off-road work. Again, these lights were developed for racing: for nighttime sports-car races such as Le Mans, where a driver needs to see at speeds in excess of 200 mph. These powerful lights soon proved their worth in off-road racing.

The most popular driving lights employ quartz-iodide elements that throw a brilliant white beam more than a mile. The shape of the beam is controlled by the lens fluting. The beam can be narrowed for long-distance probing or fanned out for fog penetration. It is a shame that these fine lighting instruments are illegal on U.S. roads.

Pencil-beam, long-distance lights are usually mounted on the roof of the vehicle or on the top of the roll bar to give an even greater range. One drawback is that dust can refract and scatter the beam, blinding the driver. To combat this problem, off-pavement racers developed the "sugar scoop," a curved metal sheet, usually painted flat black, to keep the light from shining down directly in front of the truck. If you look carefully at the accompanying photos, you will notice small sugar scoops mounted under and in front of the lights.

ALL-WHEEL DRIVE

All right, so accessories have purpose other than image-building. What's so great about four-wheel drive? Why pay for a second driving axle, to carry it around, put up with the harsh ride, and stand for the maintenance? In a word—mobility.

A four-wheel drive pickup, armed with winch and shod with high-flotation tires, can go almost anywhere on this continent. New vistas open, from the boulder-strewn passes of the high Rockies to the green jungles of Louisianna bayou country.

4WD VARIATIONS

Until a few years ago there was only one type of commercial four-wheel drive—part time. On the pavement the front axle idled. When the driver wanted to leave the road, he engaged the front axle by means of a lever in the cab.

There are several good reasons why part-time 4WD cannot be engaged on the pavement. The most significant of these is the difference in speed between the front and rear axles.

In a sharp turn, the rear wheels leave the track of the front wheels. In other words, the front and rear axles rotate at slightly different speeds. The same phenomenon occurs when the vehicle is driven in a straight line. You can verify this by marking the tires at the 12 o'clock position with chalk and driving a few hundred feet. The chalk marks will array randomly, showing that the wheels on each axle moved a different distance (compensated for by the axle differential) and that each axle set moved independently of the other. Variations in tire pressure and rolling diameter, as well as in the road surface, account for this. That the axles do not turn the same speed hardly matters in the dirt, since vehicle speeds are low and the tires have opportunity to slip.

On the pavement there can be little tire slip. Yet with both wheel sets under power, axle speeds *must* be identical. The drive shaft, caught between antagonistic gear sets, winds and unwinds like a torsion bar. Within a few miles the shaft snaps or, what is more likely, the transfer-case gears fail.

In addition, many four-wheel drive vehicles ran their front and rear axles at different ratios. While this was not desirable,

Fig. 16-2. A 4WD truck from Chevrolet—the K30 with a 1-ton load rating. The K30 is intended primarily for 4WD enthusiasts who want to mount a camper.

it was convenient for the manufacturer who purchased front and rear axle assemblies from different suppliers.

Today there is an alternative—full-time four-wheel drive. By incorporating a differential in the transfer case, engineers at Borg-Warner and New Process were able to make full-time four-wheel drive a reality. Full-time 4WD offers real advantages for cars and trucks. With all wheels engaged, the vehicle is safer under most conditions, particularly when the road surface is slick with rain, mud, or ice. Cornering is much more stable. Nor do you have to stop and engage the front axle before you venture off the pavement. At first there was resistance to full-time 4WD. For years owners had been cautioned against driving on the pavement with the front axle engaged, and they were wary of the new systems. Acceptance came slowly, and some owners are not yet convinced. But now, most people accept the concept and most manufacturers offer full-time 4WD. Jeep uses the Borg-Warner Quadra-Trac system and Ford, Chevrolet, GMC, and Chrysler use the New Process sytem. Only International is without the full-time option.

CHEVROLET

Chevrolet identifies its 4WD pickups with the letter K. The K20 has a 3/4-ton rating and the K30, new for 1977, is a one-tonner (Fig. 16-2). These pickups can be ordered with rubber mats and without headliner or as fancy as the customer wants, complete with power windows, power door locks, air conditioning, and stereo tape deck. The factories have come to realize that four-wheel drive trucks need not be spartan.

Dodge

All-wheel drive pickups from Dodge carry a famous name—Power Wagon (Fig. 16-3). During World War II, Power Wagons achieved a fame almost equal to the Jeep. Dodge offers four-wheel drive in trucks with three GVW (gross vehicle weight) ratings in what are commonly called 1/2-ton, 3/4-ton and 1-ton sizes. They are, respectively, the W100, W200, and W300. Since the Chrysler Corporation owns New Process Gear, all Dodge production uses New Process full-time four-wheel drive.

Ford

Ford offers two 4WD pickups: the F-150 and the F-250. The 5/8-ton F150 features coil springs at the front. Competetive

Fig. 16-3. The Power Wagon reflects the 60 years of experience Dodge has had in building 4WD trucks.

drive vechicles use leaf springs or torsion bars. The F-250 is the high-strutting 3/4 ton pickup you always notice. It stands tallest in the industry. In mid-1977, Ford made major changes to the F-250; dropping the overall height 2 1/2 inches while, at the same time, increasing the ground clearance 0.7 inch. Payload jumped 560 lb., and the turn circle was reduced.

Jeep

The Jeep Corporation, best known for their CJ series, manufactures a trio of fine pickups: the J10, J20, and J30. The numbers refer to the GVW rating. Jeep trucks feature

Fig. 16-4. Jeep pickups are tough, and the modish Honcho is no exception. It comes from the factory with spoked wheels, white-letter tires, side trim, and blue denim seat covers.

Fig. 16-5. International offers this little 4WD pickup called the Terra. Despite its compact dimensions, it can carry loads up to 2400 lb. This Terra is decked out in Feather trim.

Borg-Warner Quadra-Trac full-time four-wheel drive. A styled version of the J-10, called the Honcho, is shown in Fig. 16-4.

International Harvester

IH offers a compact pickup known as the Terra (Fig. 16-5). It can be ordered with a fiberglass or cloth top, making it the only convertible pickup built in the U.S. The Terra has a good load-carrying capacity and has proven to be a tough little critter with a surprisingly good payload capacity. Like the rest of the industry, IH has responded to customer demand by offering a trim package that includes paint, larger tires, wider wheels, driving lights, and push bar.

4WD MINIS

Not one Japanese manufacturer makes a 4WD mini-pickup. But thanks to West Coast enterprise, more and more all-wheel drive minis are hitting the roads and trails these days (Fig. 16-6). Customizers take a stock mini and transform it into an all-terrain terror—that still delivers the gas mileage.

What is involved is the installation of a front-drive axle and a transfer case (Fig. 16-7). Fortunately, the drive axle from a

Fig. 16-6. This 4WD Datsun can go just about anywhere it's pointed.

133

Fig. 16-7. Converting mini-trucks to four-wheel drive has become an assembly-line operation.

Fig. 16-8. The first step in the conversion removing the original front suspension. The upper and lower A-arms, coil springs, and the spindles are discarded. In many conversions, the disc brake is adapted to the 4WD axle.

Fig. 16-9. Once the suspension components are removed, brackets for the front drive axle are welded into place.

Jeep CF, a Dana 30, is the right width. The original front suspension is discarded and replaced by the live Dana axle, supported on leaf springs (Figs. 16-8 through 16-10). Spring mounts are welded to the frame (Fig. 16-11).

Fig. 16-10. A neat installation.

Fig. 16-11. The front-spring bracket is an example of the quality of workmanship in this project.

In most cases disc brakes from the original front end are retained by adapting them to the new drive axle (Fig. 16-12). The stock steering box is also retained. However, steering links must be designed and fabricated. The designer must not deviate from the original steering geometry, or complications, such as roll steer and bump steer (steering inputs caused by body roll and suspension movement),will appear. This is not a project for an amateur.

The Jeep transfer case, a Dana 20, is used. It is a two-speed case design that supplies power to the front axle and gives 2:1 reduction gearing for rough going. The transfer case is mounted aft of the transmission and shifted by a lever in the passenger compartment (Figs. 16-13 and 16-14).

To install the transfer case, the converter fabricates mounts that are welded to the frame. When the transfer case is installed, a driveshaft, also specially fabricated, is run to the front axle.

In addition to these major modifications, there are some minor changes that add performance. In order to fit larger tires, the ride height of the truck must be raised. This is done by the use of blocks between spring eyes and the chassis (Fig. 6-15).

But no matter how high one raises the body, ground clearance is still determined by the differentials that are only 8 inches or so from the ground. It is prudent to fit skid plates and axle trusses.

Fig. 16-12. Disc brakes are fadeproof and almost immune to water.

Fig. 16-13. The transfer case mounts aft of the gearbox, where it is engaged by the lever on the right.

Fig. 16-14. In addition to 4WD, this mini features air conditioning and CB.

Fig. 16-15. Springs are mounted on extended brackets to raise the body.

Mini-pickups have unique advantages: compact size, simple four-cylinder engines, good fuel economy, moderate first cost, and the ability to negotiate narrow trails are a few.

Chapter 17

Custom Paint

Custom paint can mean the most radical, diamond-dusted, acetylene-smoked, mural-bedecked, flame-licked, LSD-inspired finish, one that makes even gas-pump jockeys drop their jaws in momentary wonder. Or it can mean a careful reproduction of the original color, with a cautious foray into pin-striping or highlight-toning. The result is a conservative paint job, but one that puts the whammy on anything that rolls out of a Detroit spray booth.

Automotive paint is expensive and in recent years has become more so. But the real cost of custom paint is the labor, some of it highly skilled, most of it donkey work. This situation makes it possible for an amateur to save money by doing at least part of the work himself. A really ambitious (or dollar-shy) amateur can rent an air compressor and do the whole thing—if he keeps a respectful distance from the really exotic finishes.

PAINTS

Automotive paint is mixed in five basic formulations, each with unique advantages and annoyances.

Synthetic Enamel

Synthetic enamel is the automotive version of oil-base house and barn paint. It is the least exotic of automotive finishes, but one that is relatively inexpensive, easy to apply, and fairly durable. There is no serious problem about spraying synthetic over other finishes and it retains flexibility for years.

Off-roaders sometimes use it, figuring that the best that can be said of any off-road paint is that it stops rust. But no serious customizer touches the stuff: it is subject to dust and insect damage for four hours after spraying and does not forgive mistakes easily. A run means the whole panel must be wiped down and resprayed.

Acrylic Enamel

Acrylic enamel is the most popular finish with auto manufacturers and with the aftermarket. Acrylic dries relatively fast, is quite durable, and can be had in all truck colors. However, more than a little skill is needed to apply it.

Cellulose Lacquer

The terms lacquer and enamel represent two families of paint. While there are fundamental chemical differences between the two, as far as the painter is concerned, the big difference is in the way the paints dry. Enamels dry by oxidation, from the outside first. Lacquer solidifies as the thinner evaporates, the coat hardening at once.

Any novice will make mistakes (and any honest professional will admit that he does too). The panel must, of course, be dry before sanding and reshooting. With enamel, appearances can be illusive; the paint may appear hard and smear once the sandpaper breaks through the oxidized "skin." Lacquer dries in a piece. If it appears hard, it is hard. And because of its rapid drying time, there is less tendency for lacquer to run.

Cellulose lacquer was introduced in 1927 under the Du Pont trade name, Duco. For many years it was the only automotive spray paint. It remains the easiest to apply—you can do acceptable work with a spray gun attachment to a vacuum cleaner—and the most forgiving. Applied with professional equipment and skill, cellulose lacquer gives an unrivaled gloss and depth. Since mistakes are easy to correct, the completed job can have zero defects.

But Duco and similar paints have long been obsoleted. Too much labor is involved in compounding, or rubbing out, the finish. However, at least one firm continues to market cellulose lacquer, but only in black and white for prestige vehicles.

Acrylic Lacquer

Acrylic lacquer can be thought of as a compromise between synthetic enamel and cellulose lacquer. The finish is glossy as sprayed and, while compounding enhances the appearance, it is not absolutely necessary. Drying time is short and mistakes can be undone fairly easily.

On the debit side, acrylic lacquer is more expensive than either type of enamel and gives less coverage. While two coats of enamel are sufficient, seven, nine, or even 27 coats of lacquer are applied, with time-consuming hand sanding between each. But the translucence of lacquer gives the finish a deep gloss with none of the "just-painted" rawness of enamel.

Epoxy

Two-part epoxy paints proved themselves on ocean-going ships. Traditional synthetic enamels require constant care in a salt-water environment, care that consumes most of the energies of the deck crews. A ship painted with epoxy is safe from corrosion for five years. Commercial airlines were the next customers, followed by long-distance truckers, and street rodders.

But epoxy is expensive—averaging $40 a gallon—and for best results should be applied over bare metal.

PAINT SYSTEMS

The color coat is the final link of a chemical chain that starts with the metal conditioner (a weak acid solution used to clean and give tooth to bare metal). Each of the paints mentioned above—synthetic enamel, acrylic enamel, cellulose lacquer, acrylic lacquer, and epoxy—requires its own thinner or reducer and primer. Mixing elements between paint systems is asking for trouble.

Unless the truck is stripped down to bare metal, it is safer to build on the original paint system. For example, General Motors trucks built before 1958 were painted with cellulose lacquer, and cellulose should be used as the refinishing agent. Later GM production requires acrylic lacquer. Ford and Chrysler favor acrylic enamel. Your paint dealer will be able to give you specific recommendations.

EQUIPMENT

The quality of the work will reflect the quality of the equipment.

Spray Guns

Bleeder guns vent air when the trigger is released, and are intended to operate from small, tankless compressors.

Professional spray guns are the nonbleeder type, holding air in the line and tank when idle. A second distinction is the method of paint feed. Pressure-feed guns deliver the paint under air pressure; siphon-feed guns depend upon a vacuum generated across the nozzle, like a flit gun. Most auto painters prefer siphon feed for the superior control it gives.

In airless guns the paint is subjected to tremendous pressure by a self-contained pump and forced out through a tiny aperture. The spray pattern is adjusted by changing aperture number and shape. The fact that these guns eliminate the cost of a compressor and the bother of air lines makes them attractive. Unfortunately, these guns do not give the control of professional air guns. The $90 or so that one costs would be best put toward a better outfit.

Compressors

The compressor should be capable of supplying 8.5 cubic feet of air a minute. This means that the compressor and the motor to drive it are prohibitively expensive for a home craftsman who may paint only two or three vehicles in his lifetime. Obviously, the compressor should be rented.

Figure 17-1 illustrates a professional installation, intended for volume work. The most important element in the drawing is the air regulator shown at the extreme right. If the rental compressor is not equipped with an air regulator (also known

SUGGESTED INSTALLATION OF AIR COMPRESSOR AND OIL AND WATER EXTRACTOR

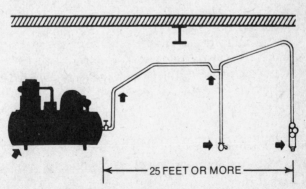

25 FEET OR MORE

Fig. 17-1. A professional air-compressor installation. Note the drain plug and air regulator. (Courtesy Martin Senour.)

as an oil and water extractor), it would be wise to purchase one. The regulator gives better control of tank pressure, muffles pressure surges, and eliminates most water and oil contamination.

Respirator

Paint fumes—especially epoxy—are toxic. Obtain a good quality respirator, rated for industrial use. Wear it whenever you are using a spray gun, or for that matter, a grinder. In addition, the spray area should be vented.

PANEL PREPARATION

All paint jobs, even the most exotic, begin with gallons of elbow grease. Any flaws in the metalwork—flaws that were insignificant or even invisible under the original paint—will be emphasized by the color coats.

Sanding

The basic technique of panel finishing is block sanding. Automotive paint houses sell hard-rubber sanding blocks, sized to accept quarter sheets of wet-or-dry abrasive. This abrasive paper is available in various grades, beginning at the fine end of the spectrum with No. 600. Grit No. 220 is almost pebbly in texture and is intended for reducing rust deposits and weld flash. Most automotive sanding is confined to the 300 grits.

Wet-or-dry abrasive works best under a trickle of water, particularly when sanding paint. A sanding block cannot, of course, be used on sharply curved surfaces. Hold the abrasive with your fingers at right angles to the direction of stroke. If the lie of your fingers parallels the stroke, the work surface will be streaked.

Sand the entire truck. Where bare metal shows, carefully featheredge the surrounding paint, using finer and finer grades of abrasive to smooth the transition between steel and paint. If you do the work right, you will clearly see a ring of primer, then possibly a sealer coat, and finally a cross section of color.

Removing Paint

The best way to remove all of the old finish is to have the vehicle sand blasted by a professional who has had experience with automotive sheet-metal. Sand blasting leaves the metal in perfect condition for priming. Nor is there any chance of wax or chemical residue remaining on the bare metal. However, special care is needed to shield glass and chrome.

Grinding is the second alternative, and may be the favored one if the truck body has been repaired with plastic filler. Use a high-speed grinder and nonclog, open-coat discs (Fig. 17-2).

Paint remover, such as Martin Senour No. 6801 Paint Blitz, may also be used, although nobody promised you a rose garden with it. Factory baked-on finishes are stubborn and require repeated applications before they blister and bubble. All of the paint remover must be flushed off the truck, or it will continue its work on the new finish.

Once the paint is removed, bare metal should be treated with Martin Senour No. 6879 Twin Etch or the equivalent before priming.

Filling

Body putty can be used to fill superficial blemishes—blemishes that are no deeper than the paint. Gouges and dents respond better to one of the two-part epoxy fillers. These fillers, known variously as "mud," or Snowhite or Bondo (after two trade names), make a permanent, almost undetectable repair. But apply fillers with discretion. Mud is no substitute for hammer and dolly work. As a rule its use should be limited to dents that are a quarter-inch or less deep. Apply the filler over bare metal that has been rough ground.

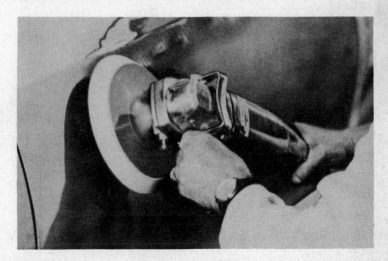

Fig. 17-2. A disc grinder is a painter's best friend. (Courtesy Martin Senour.)

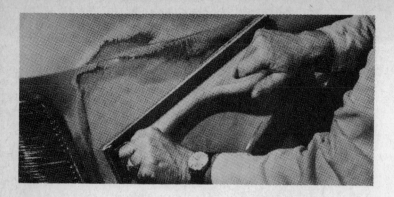

Fig. 17-3. Use a body (or Surform) file to contour plastic filler while it is still soft. Sand when the filler hardens. (Courtesy Martin Senour.)

Mix according to directions on the can. When thoroughly mixed, press the filler onto the work surface. Most professionals use a plastic squeegee, although you can get fair results with a putty knife. Allow the filler to become semihard, a process that should take 10–20 minutes, depending upon the temperature and how much catalyst you used. Before it is firmed, shape with a body file (Fig. 17-3). Once the filler hardens, finish with a sanding block. If you use a grinder for rough finishing, wear a respirator. The dust is hazardous.

Masking

The less you mask, the better. In other words, remove the trim, bumpers, and light assemblies. Tape off the windows (using butcher paper or multiple layers of newsprint), door-lock cylinders, and trim that is too stubborn to remove. Cover the tires and wheels with cardboard shields.

Apply the tape to a clean, dry surface, using the narrowest width that gives complete coverage. Do not stretch the tape except on curved surfaces. Remove as soon as the paint is no longer vulnerable to dust damage.

PAINTING

Wipe the vehicle down with Martin Senour No. 6383 Kleanz-Easy or the equivalent to remove fingerprints and contamination left by silicone-based waxes and polishes. Once clean, do not touch the surface with your bare hands.

Stir the primer-surfacer, strain it, and mix with the appropriate thinner or reducer in the proportion suggested by the manufacturer. Accuracy is important.

Fig. 17-4. The gun must be held 90° to the work surface. When spraying horizontal panels, loop the air line over your shoulder and stop the cup vent with a rag.

The spray gun should be held at a distance of 6—8 inches from the work surface and at right angles to it (Fig. 17-4). When painting horizontal surfaces hold the gun with the nozzle pointed straight down. A rag over the vent hole will prevent dribbles. As with all repetitive work, rhythm is important. Move the gun with your arm and shoulder so it remains the same distance from the work throughout the stroke (Fig. 17-5).

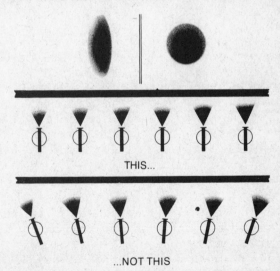

THIS...

...NOT THIS

Fig. 17-5. Keep the nozzle the same distance from, and at right angles to, the panel throughout the stroke. Trigger the gun before the stroke begins and release the trigger at the end of the stroke. (Courtesy Martin Senour.)

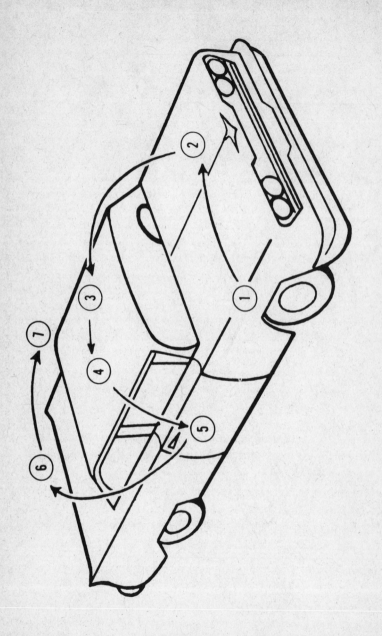

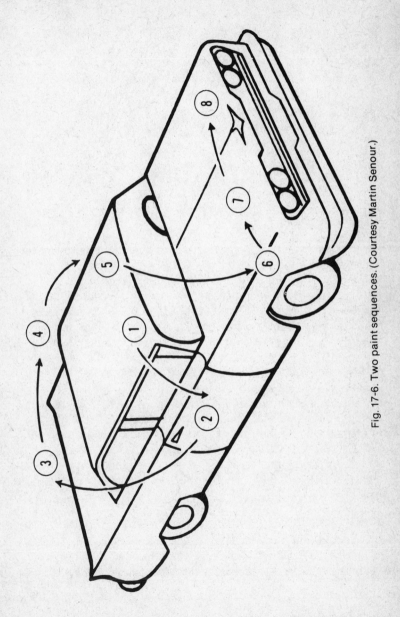

Fig. 17-6. Two paint sequences. (Courtesy Martin Senour.)

Fig. 17-7. Here is an all-time favorite—flames. A most effective treatment against a dark background.

Most professionals trigger the gun, pressing it at the beginning of the stroke and releasing it at the end.

Enamel should be fogged on in light, "kiss" coats so the film progressively becomes thicker. Shooting a coat of enamel requires that you walk around the truck three or four times. Lacquer has less of a tendency to run and is laid on fairly heavy. One time around the truck should give complete coverage.

Spray the door jambs first...cut the air pressure to 20 psi and adjust the nozzle to give a round spray pattern to eliminate overspray on the upholstery. Close the door as far as the first detent on the door hold so that it does not stick shut. Raise the pressure to 50 psi and shoot the underside of the hood and trunk lid. Follow either of the sequences shown in Fig. 17-6.

Allow the primer-surfacer to dry, sand, and shoot the color coats.

CUSTOM PAINTS

Custom paints are, for the most part, simple elaborations of monocolors. The basic skills are the same, but the visual dramatics of these finishes demand the highest level of competence. Step gingerly into custom painting, and then only after you have mastered the basics. Figures 17-7 through 17-15 illustrate the kind of custom painting popular now.

Fig. 17-8. A close-up of the pickup shown in the previous photo. Note the flame pattern and way the colors are blended.

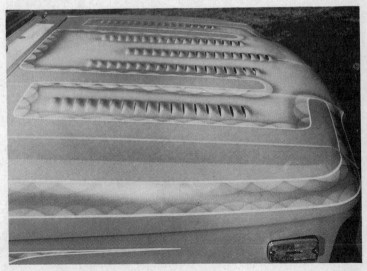

Fig. 17-9. Another old-time treatment making a comeback—louvers. These louvers are highlighted by the paint pattern.

Fig. 17-10. An eagle on the hood. Airbrush artistry is popular on newer pickups.

Fig. 17-11. This mini is a rolling advertisement for its owner, a custom painter. It features a little bit of everything.

Fig. 17-12. A Datsun high-boy custom paint over the factory base coat.

Fig. 17-13. Designs such as these are produced by misting the paint over cardboard templates.

Fig. 17-14. This GMC sports a toned and patterned beltline.

Fig. 17-15. The base paint frames the custom-finished panel, an effect achieved with quarter-inch masking tape. If the owner would remove the black paint from the headlight rings, he would discover that the factory chromed them.

Index